AUSTRALIA

The Lucky Country

COOKBOOK

PA-R
PRODUCTIONS

ACKNOWLEDGEMENT LIST

We would like to thank the following for their assistance
in the compilation of this book:
Tourism Commission of New South Wales
Queensland Tourist and Travel Corporation
Victorian Tourism Commission
Tourism Tasmania
Western Australian Tourist Centre
South Australian Government Travel Centre

Cookery Editor
Loukie Werle
Food Stylist
Wendy Berecry
Assistants
Lucy Kelly, Belinda Warn, Fionnala Lagan, Barbara Tucker
Photography
Warren Webb
Photography Credits
Gary Lewis
*(cover; pages 20-21, 34-35, 50-51, 122-123, 130-131,
200-201, 202-203, 204-205, 252-253)*
Art Director
Stephen Joseph
Editorial Production
Margaret Gore & Associates
Design Director
Craig Osment
Editorial Director
Philip Gore
Typesetting
APT Pty Ltd
Print Production
Griffin Press, Netley, South Australia
Published
*by Peter Antill-Rose & Associates Pty Ltd, Unit 8, 10 Anella Avenue,
Castle Hill, NSW 2154, Australia, in association with
Century Magazines, 216-224 Commonwealth Street, Surry Hills,
NSW 2010, Australia.*

ISBN NO. 1 875216 01 4

CONTENTS

The *Lucky Country Cookbook* is a celebration of this wonderful country and the rich variety of food it produces. From the tropical north to the rich dairy pastures of temperate Tasmania, from the wheat fields of New South Wales to the beef of the golden West, Australians have a never-ending choice of wonderful food produce.

Earlier this century, Australian food was rather dull. We didn't have a national style of cooking, only a bastard form of British cookery, which never enjoyed the same reputation as French or Italian.

The crops we grew were virtually the same as those from the British Isles and roast meat with three boiled vegetables was our standard fare.

Not until after World War II, when an influx of migrants from other European countries brought their own style of cooking and produce to this country, did Australia begin to develop its palate.

Restaurants sprang up offering new and exciting cuisines and this inspired the home cook to try the new dishes. Soon there was a demand for continental cuts of meat and vegetables, tropical fruits were brought down from the north and strange looking cheeses began to appear in our stores.

Today, Australia can boast the finest food in the world, whether cooked at home or in a restaurant. In this book we look at this marvellous land, its produce and the recipes that have become part of our national cuisine.

FRUITS OF THE SEA

Australia, perhaps more than any other place in the world, enjoys an amazing variety of locally caught seafood. Our extensive coastline provides us with vast fisheries that yield fish and shellfish that are the envy of the world. Indeed, certain areas are quite famous for their own particular specialty: Queensland's mudcrabs and barramundi, the oysters, bream and flathead of New South Wales, crayfish of South Australia and Tasmania's trout and salmon to name but a few.

Fish falls into two main categories; fat/oily and lean/dry. Fat/oily fish are excellent for grilling, barbecuing and baking, with species such as tuna, mullet, tailor and mackerel being particularly delicious. Lean/dry fish include bream, flathead, snapper and john dory. They are superb for steaming, poaching or pan frying, although you can grill or bake them with good results if kept moist.

And of course Australian shellfish such as crab, prawns, oysters, scallops, lobster and mussels are amongst the best in the world.

Seafood is also a very important part of our diet, high in protein and rich in vitamins and minerals. Fish also is much lower in fat than meat although remember not to use too much oil or fat if grilling.

Become familiar with the fish available in your local fish shop and enjoy the rich bounty of our seas.

Grilled Swordfish with Mustard-Shallot Butter

1 tblspn coarse grain mustard

4 tblspn butter

1 large shallot, finely chopped

¼ tspn salt

pepper

4 swordfish steaks, 185g (6oz) each

2 tblspn oil

1 Combine mustard, butter, shallots, salt and pepper. Mix well.

2 Dry fillets on paper towels, brush with 1 tablespoon oil. Brush griller tray with 1 tablespoon oil. Grill about 3 minutes on each side, or until cooked when tested.

3 Place fish on heated plates. Place 1 tablespoon of the butter mixture on each steak and quickly run under the griller to start butter melting. Serve hot.

Serves 4

Whisky Cream Lobster

2 cooked lobsters

30g (1oz) butter

4 spring onions (scallions), chopped

⅓ cup whisky

2 tspn cornflour

1 tblspn lemon juice

½ cup cream

½ cup sour cream

1 tblspn chopped parsley

2 tspn grated lemon rind

1 Cut lobsters, down the back, lengthwise in half. Remove grey stomach sac and back vein. Remove meat in 1 piece, cut into bite-sized pieces. Wash meat and shell, drain well.

2 Melt butter in a frying pan, add spring onions and whisky, cook until whisky reduces to 2 tablespoons. Stir in blended cornflour, lemon juice, cream and sour cream, bring to a boil, reduce heat to low. Stir in lobster meat, cook until heated through.

3 Spoon meat and sauce back into lobster shells. Sprinkle with combined parsley and lemon rind.

Serves 4

P.2-3: The QEII glides past the Sydney Opera House to her berth at Circular Quay. P.4-5: The rich pastures of western Victoria near the Grampian Mountains. P.8-9: The famous old church at Lightning Ridge. P.10: A quaint antique shop in Berry, New South Wales. P.12-13: The beautiful Erskine Falls near Lorne in Victoria. P.14: Succulent seafood fare from Queensland. Right: The untouched rainforests of tropical Queensland.

Whisky Cream Lobster

Sardines Baked with Potatoes and Sun-dried Tomatoes

4 tblspn oil

4 potatoes, sliced finely

2 onions, sliced finely

salt

pepper

¼ cup sun-dried tomatoes with their oil

8 fresh sardines, cleaned

½ cup white wine

1 tspn thyme

lemon wedges

¼ cup chopped parsley

1 Put 2 tablespoons of the oil in an ovenproof dish large enough to hold the fish in one layer. Arrange the potatoes in one layer. Cover with the onions, season with salt and pepper. Chop tomatoes, reserving oil, and tuck in between the onion and potato. Pour over reserved oil. Cover and bake in 180°C (350°F) oven for 40 minutes.

2 Dry sardines on paper towels. Place on top of potato, onion and tomato mixture. Pour wine over fish and season with salt and lots of freshly ground black pepper, sprinkle over the thyme and 2 tablespoons oil. Return to oven and bake for 15 minutes. Serve hot from the dish, garnished with lemon wedges and chopped parsley.

Serves 4

Sauteed Tuna with Avocado Cream

4 tuna steaks, 185g (6oz) each

4 tblspn butter

2 tblspn spring onion (scallion), chopped

1 cup cream

2 tblspn mashed avocado

Tabasco

salt

pepper

parsley sprigs

1 Cook tuna steaks in 2 table-spoons butter till just done. Straight away remove from pan and arrange on serving platter. Keep warm.

2 Add remaining butter to frying pan, add spring onion and cook gently for 1 minute. Add cream and avocado, season lightly with a few drops of Tabasco, salt and pepper, boil and reduce by half. Correct seasoning.

3 Pour sauce over fish and serve garnished with some parsley sprigs.

Serves 4

Devilled Crab Bake

2 x 200g (6½oz) can crabmeat

60g (2oz) butter

2 onions, chopped

2 red capsicum (pepper), chopped

2 sticks celery, sliced

3 cloves garlic, crushed

½ cup mayonnaise

1 tblspn Worcestershire sauce

2 tblspn fruit chutney

2 tblspn chopped parsley

½ cup fresh white breadcrumbs

30g (1oz) butter, extra

¼ tspn paprika

1 Drain and flake crabmeat. Melt butter in a frying pan, add onion, capsicum, celery and garlic, stir over low heat until vegetables are tender.

2 Stir in crab, mayonnaise, Worcestershire sauce, chutney and parsley. Spoon into four 1-cup serving dishes.

3 Combine breadcrumbs, melted butter and paprika, sprinkle over crab mixture, bake in moderate oven for 15 minutes or until golden brown and heated through.

Serves 4

Right: The wonderful oysters of the Hawkesbury River, just north of Sydney. P.20-21: Tranquil Brampton Island on the Great Barrier Reef.

Left: Devilled Crab Bake.

Orange Roughy Fillets with Cucumber Sauce

1 tblspn butter, softened

¼ cup onion, finely chopped

750g (1½lb) orange roughy (sea perch, striped bass) fillets, skinned

¾ cup white wine

2 cucumbers, peeled, seeded, cut into 1cm (½in) cubes

1 cup fish stock

⅔ cup cream

2 tblspn chopped parsley

salt

pepper

1 Brush butter into baking dish large enough to hold fish in one layer, sprinkle with onion, add fish, season with salt and freshly ground black pepper.

2 Add wine, cucumber and stock, cover with foil and cook in 200°C (400°F) oven about 20 minutes or until fish is cooked when tested. Remove fish with slotted spoon to serving platter, keep warm.

3 Pour cooking liquid and cucumber into saucepan and cook over high heat till liquid thickens. Add cream, cook till sauce thickens, stir in parsley, season with salt and freshly ground black pepper. Pour over fish fillets, serve hot.

Serves 4

Smoked Salmon Moulds with Fresh Tomato Sauce

375g (¾lb) very thinly sliced smoked salmon

½ cup thickened cream, beaten stiff

2 tblspn red caviar

¼ tspn cayenne pepper

4 tomatoes, peeled, seeded and chopped

salt

pepper

⅓ cup chopped chives

1 Line 4 deep moulds, 8cm (3in) across the top, with smoked salmon slices. Trim away any overhanging bits, puree these and any leftover smoked salmon in food processor.

2 Combine stiffly beaten cream with caviar, cayenne pepper and pureed smoked salmon, stuff into moulds. Cover, place in refrigerator for 2 hours at least.

3 Puree tomatoes in food processor, season with salt and freshly ground pepper. Loosen salmon moulds running a thin knife around the inside, invert moulds smartly onto plates, surround with tomato sauce, scatter sauce with chives. Serve cold.

Serves 4

Left: Seals sun themselves on a beach in South Australia. Above: A traditional Queensland house in Brisbane.

Snapper Fillet Parcels

Mediterranean Mixed Seafood Gratin

750g (1½lb) firm-fleshed white fish fillets

250g (½lb) prawns (shrimp)

250g (½lb) scallops

2 leeks, sliced, white part only

1 large onion, sliced

2 cloves garlic

3 potatoes, peeled and cut into 1cm (½in) cubes

¼ cup olive oil

¼ cup black olives, chopped

½ cup dry white wine

¼ cup chopped parsley

salt

pepper

½ cup fresh breadcrumbs

½ cup Parmesan cheese, grated

2 tblspn butter, melted

1 In a large frying pan cook the leeks, onion, garlic, potatoes in oil over a moderate heat till potatoes are just tender.

2 Add olives, wine, parsley, season with salt and pepper and transfer the mixture to an ovenproof dish which can hold the fish in one layer. Arrange the fish fillets on top and add the prawns and scallops, fitting them in between the fillets.

3 Combine breadcrumbs, cheese and butter in a bowl, mix well and place this mixture over the seafood. Place in moderate 180°C (350°F) oven and bake till golden brown on top and fish flakes when tested. Serve immediately.

Serves 4

Snapper Fillet Parcels

4 large snapper (sea bass, red snapper) fillets

2 sheets ready-rolled puff pastry

4 slices tomato

1 egg, beaten

FILLING

1 tblspn oil

1 onion, thinly sliced

2 tspn grated lemon rind

1 tblspn chopped parsley

8 black olives, chopped

1 Make filling first: Heat oil in a frying pan, add onion, stir-fry until tender, drain on absorbent paper. Combine onion with lemon rind, parsley and olives.

2 Remove skin and bones from fish fillets, cut each fillet cross-wise in half. Cut pastry sheets in half to give 4 rectangles.

3 Place half a fillet onto centre of one rectangle of pastry. Top with one quarter of the filling and a slice of tomato. Top with half a fish fillet.

4 Brush edges of pastry with a little water, bring edges together to form a parcel, pressing together well to seal completely. Repeat with remaining ingredients to give 4 parcels.

5 Place parcels seam side down on a greased baking tray. Decorate with extra pastry cut into leaf shapes if desired. Cut 2 vents in each to allow steam to escape. Brush with beaten egg, bake in medium hot oven for 5 minutes. Reduce heat to moderate, bake further 15 minutes or until golden brown.

Serves 4

Scallops with Mushrooms and Tomatoes

3 tblspn olive oil

1 tblspn butter

750g (1½lb) scallops

flour

1 tblspn olive oil, extra

3 tblspn butter, extra

3 tblspn onion, finely chopped

125g (4oz) mushrooms, sliced

2 tblspn chopped fresh basil

salt

pepper

½ cup white wine

1 cup tomato, peeled, seeded and chopped

2 cloves garlic, crushed

2 tblspn chopped parsley

1 Combine oil and butter in frying pan, dust scallops with flour, shake off excess, season with salt and pepper and cook till firm to the touch. Remove to bowl.

2 Heat extra butter and oil in frying pan, cook onion 1 minute, add mushrooms, basil and salt and freshly ground black pepper. Cook 3 minutes.

3 Add wine, reduce mixture over high heat by half. Add tomato and juices accumulated in scallop bowl, reduce liquid till thick, stirring constantly.

4 Add scallops and garlic, heat through, add parsley. Serve hot.

Serves 4

Below: The remnants of a sandstone church built by early South Australian settlers. P.26-27: Morning light greets a fishing fleet on the south coast of New South Wales.

Baked Pearl Perch Fillets

8 spring onions (scallions), chopped

4 pearl perch (red mullet, black seabass) fillets, 185g (6oz) each

salt

pepper

juice of 1 lemon

1/3 cup chopped mushroom

1 cup chopped tomatoes

1/2 cup chopped parsley

1/2 cup dry white wine

150ml (1/4 pint) sour cream

1 Place spring onions in baking dish. Season with a little salt. Arrange fillets in one layer on top, season with salt and freshly ground pepper, pour over lemon juice, scatter with mushrooms, tomatoes and parsley.

2 Pour over wine, cover with foil, bake in 180°C (350°F) oven till fish is cooked when tested, about 20–30 minutes. Remove from oven, pour off liquid into saucepan. Keep fish warm.

3 Add sour cream to fish liquid, bring to a boil and cook till slightly thickened and reduced. Place fish on heated serving plates, pour over sauce, serve hot.

Serves 4

Gemfish Kebabs with Apple Marinade

750g (1½lb) gemfish (sea bream, orange roughy) fillets

3/4 cup apple juice

2 tspn ground cumin

2 tspn grated fresh ginger

2 cloves garlic, crushed

1 red chilli, chopped

1 cucumber

340g (11oz) can sliced pineapple, drained

bamboo skewers

1 Remove skin from gemfish, cut into 3cm (1¼ in) cubes. Combine gemfish with apple juice, cumin, ginger, garlic and chilli, cover, refrigerate at least 1 hour, drain, reserve marinade.

2 Cut cucumber in half lengthwise, scoop out seeds, cut into chunks the same size as the fish. Cut pineapple slices into 3.

3 Thread gemfish onto skewers alternately with cucumber and pineapple. Cook under preheated grill until gemfish is tender, brush occasionally with reserved marinade.

Serves 4

Below: River boats cruise the Gordon River in the southern wilderness areas of Tasmania.

Gemfish Kebabs with Apple Marinade.

Whiting Fillets in Lemon Coconut Sauce

750g (1½lb) whiting fillets

2 tblspn butter

3 tblspn lemon juice

2 tblspn lemon rind, grated

¼ tspn nutmeg, grated

½ tspn salt

1½ tblspn coconut cream

1 Melt butter, add lemon juice, lemon rind, nutmeg and salt. Add whiting fillets and cook gently with lid on frying pan till fish is barely cooked.

2 When very nearly cooked, add coconut cream and stir till thickening. Place fish on heated platter and serve immediately with the sauce.

Serves 4

Atlantic Salmon Fillets in Red Radish-Dill Mousseline Sauce

12 red radishes

4 tblspn finely chopped dill

1 tblspn prepared strong horseradish

1½ cup mousseline sauce

1½kg (3lb) Atlantic salmon fillets

¼ cup butter

dill sprigs to garnish

1 Slice 2 radishes thinly and set aside for garnish. Finely chop remaining radishes and add to the mousseline sauce together with dill and horseradish.

2 Cook salmon fillets in butter over moderately high heat till lightly browned on both sides and just cooked in the thickest part. Season lightly with salt.

3 Divide warm mousseline sauce among six warmed plates. Place salmon fillets on top and serve hot garnished with dill sprigs and reserved radish slices.

Serves 6

Flathead with Kiwifruit

4 flathead fillets, 185g (6oz) each (angler fish, tile)

flour seasoned with salt and pepper

1 tblspn oil

1 tblspn butter

4 kiwifruit, skinned and roughly chopped

1 tblspn vermouth

salt

pepper

1 Skin flathead fillets, coat in seasoned flour, shake off excess. Heat butter with oil in frying pan till it bubbles. Add fillets, cook 2 minutes each side or until done when tested. Remove and keep warm.

2 Place kiwi fruit in food processor and blend into a paste. Pour into a saucepan and add vermouth and salt and pepper to taste. Heat gently.

3 Place flathead fillets onto warmed plates, pour kiwi sauce over and serve at once.

Serves 4

Left: The McKenzie Falls cut through the Grampians in Victoria.

Poached Sole with Lime Cream Sauce

8 sole fillets

freshly ground black pepper

¼ cup lime juice

¼ cup dry vermouth

1 tblspn tomato paste

15g (½oz) butter

⅓ cup cream

toothpicks

1 Lay sole fillets out flat, sprinkle with pepper, roll up, secure with toothpicks

2 Combine lime juice, vermouth, tomato paste and butter in a frying pan. Place fish rolls into pan, cover, simmer gently for 10 minutes or until sole is just tender. Remove sole, keep warm.

3 Add cream to sauce in frying pan, bring to the boil, reduce heat, simmer uncovered for a few minutes until sauce thickens slightly. Pour over sole to serve.

Serves 4

Anchovy and Potato Pie

3 onions, sliced

60g (2oz) butter

6 potatoes, thinly sliced

16 anchovy fillets

pepper

¾ cup cream

¼ cup finely chopped parsley

1 Fry onions in 30g (1oz) butter till golden.

2 Place one layer potatoes in buttered ovenproof dish, follow with all the onions in one layer, then all the anchovies in one layer. Finish with the remaining potatoes. Grind some black pepper over every layer.

3 Pour half of the cream over and bake in 220°C (425°F) oven, dotted with butter and bake till top is golden.

4 Pour over remaining cream and continue cooking till potatoes are tender. Serve hot sprinkled with parsley.

Serves 4

Below: Queensland koalas enjoying a feed! P.34-35: Constitution Dock in Hobart on a peaceful, summer morning.

Left: Poached Sole with Lime Cream Sauce.

36

FROM OUR SWEEPING PLAINS

As so much of our vast country is used for grazing, it is little wonder that we produce some of the best beef and lamb in the world. Cattle and sheep were brought to Australia with the First Fleeters and subsequently formed the backbone of the Australian economy. Vast cattle properties were established with the "cow cockies" pushing further and further inland – this was the age when the "beef barons" flourished. Droving became part of the fabric of the Australian way of life and "the drover's tale" entered our songs, poems, myths and legends.

Because of our droving traditions and the fact that our sheep and cattle are range-fed rather than grain-fed, Australian red meat is low in fat and high in nutritional value making it ideal for a well-balanced diet.

The Australian Meat and Livestock Corporation have also made life easier for the consumers by encouraging butchers to provide cuts of meat that are easy to prepare and delicious to eat. Try the recipes in this section to discover just how satisfying Australian meat can be.

P.36-37: The Flinders Ranges create a spectacular backdrop for Adelaide in South Australia. Left: A familiar scene at countless stockyards, this one is in Gunnedah, New South Wales.

Quick Spicy Beef and Beans

2 tspn vegetable oil

½ cup each chopped onion and green capsicum (pepper)

1 garlic clove, crushed

250g (8oz) steak, thinly sliced

1 tspn chilli powder

½ tspn curry powder

few drops pepper sauce

½ cup canned tomatoes, crushed

4 tspn tomato paste

⅔ cup canned kidney beans, drained

1 cup cooked long-grain rice, hot

1 In a 1-litre (2-pint) saucepan, heat oil, add onion, green capsicum and garlic, and saute until onion is translucent, about 5 minutes. Add veal and seasonings and cook until meat loses its pink colour, about 3 minutes.

2 Add tomatoes and tomato paste and cook, stirring occasionally, for about 5 minutes.

3 Add beans and cook until heated; serve over rice.

Serves 2

Beef Kebabs

SAUCE

¼ cup prepared barbecue sauce

8 tspn marmalade

4 tspn teriyaki or soy sauce

water

KEBABS

375g (12oz) cubed rump steak

16 cherry tomatoes

16 button mushrooms

1 **Sauce:** In a small bowl, combine barbecue sauce with marmalade and teriyaki (or soy) sauce, add water, 1 teaspoon at a time, to blend mixture to a spreading consistency using no more than 6 teaspoons.

2 **Kebabs:** On to each of eight 30 cm (12 in) skewers, thread one-eighth of the beef, 2 cherry tomatoes and 2 mushrooms, alternating ingredients. On a rack in the grilling pan, grill kebabs until meat is browned on top. Turn skewers over and grill, basting frequently with sauce, just until other side of meat is browned (do not overcook or tomatoes will split). Serve with any remaining sauce that has not been used for basting.

Serves 4

Below: An early start for this milker in Tamworth, New South Wales. Right: Riders on the old gold trails near Sofala in New South Wales.

Meatballs with Spicy Tomato Sauce

SAUCE

1 tblspn vegetable oil

1 garlic clove, crushed

½ cup each finely diced onion and green capsicum (pepper)

2 cups canned tomatoes, drained and crushed

½ cup tomato puree

½ cup water

1 cup beef stock

1½ tspn dried basil

¾ tspn salt

½ tspn each dried parsley and oregano

⅛ tspn pepper

> *Right: "The men from Snowy River", Bogong High Plains, Victoria.*

MEATBALLS

600g (1¼lb) minced veal

2 tblspn diced breadcrumbs

½ cup evaporated skimmed milk

¼ tspn garlic powder

⅛ tspn thyme

pinch each salt and pepper

1 **Sauce:** In a 2-litre (8-cup) saucepan, heat oil, add garlic, onion and pepper and saute until onion is translucent. Add remaining ingredients. Reduce heat to low, and simmer 35 minutes, stirring often.

2 **Meatballs:** In a bowl, thoroughly combine all ingredients. Shape into 4cm (1½in) balls. Transfer to large casserole dish. Bake at 190°C (375°F) for 40 minutes, or until browned. Pour sauce over meatballs and serve.

Serves 4

Crumbed Veal

3 tblspn plain dried breadcrumbs

1 tblspn plain flour

½ tspn salt

pinch pepper

4 x 150g (5oz) veal steaks

1 egg, beaten with 1½ tblspn water

3 tblspn margarine

1 On a sheet of greaseproof paper, spread the breadcrumbs and set aside.

2 In a bowl, combine flour, salt and pepper. Dredge veal in flour mixture, coating on all sides.

3 Dip each steak into beaten eggs, then into breadcrumbs, thoroughly coating all sides. In a 30cm (12in) pan over medium–high heat, heat margarine until bubbly. Add steaks and brown on both sides.

Serves 4

Meatballs with Spicy Tomato Sauce

LOW CLEARANCE
8FT 9IN 2·9 m

Minced Beef and Sausage Loaf

500g (1 lb) minced (ground) beef

2 cups soft breadcrumbs

¼ tspn salt

¼ tspn pepper

pinch dried herbs

1 medium onion, chopped

2 sticks celery, chopped finely

1 cup tomato juice

1 tspn dry mustard

1 cup evaporated milk

2 tblspn chopped parsley

250g (8oz) thin pork sausages

1 tblspn tomato sauce (catsup)

2-3 tspn cornflour

1 Mix all the ingredients together except sausages, tomato sauce and cornflour.

2 Grease loaf pan well with butter and arrange sausages side by side in the bottom. Press beef mixture over sausages in loaf pan and brush top with tomato sauce. Bake for 1–1¼ hours in moderate oven 180°C (350°F).

3 Pour the gravy off the loaf into a saucepan and thicken with 2–3 teaspoons cornflour mixed to a smooth paste with a little cold water.

4 Turn the loaf onto a heated platter. Serve in slices with the gravy and baked potatoes.

Serves 4–6

Basic Hamburgers

500g (1 lb) minced (ground) beef

1 egg yolk

pinch mixed herbs

1 large onion, chopped finely

salt and pepper

oil for frying

1 Mix the beef, egg yolk, herbs, and onion together. Season to taste with salt and pepper. Shape into 4 round flat shapes.

2 Heat oil in a frying pan. Add the hamburgers and brown quickly on one side. Turn, then brown on other side. Lower heat and continue frying until cooked evenly.

3 Serve with fresh salad (lettuce, tomato, onion) and your favourite relish on hot, toasted hamburger buns, if desired.

Serves 4

Sausage and Ham Kebabs

500 g (1 lb) small chipolata sausages

3 ham steaks, cut into cubes

440 g (14 oz) can sliced peaches, liquid reserved for marinade

12 button mushrooms

MARINADE

1 tblspn brown sugar

⅔ cup reserved peach juice

salt and pepper

1½ tspn dry mustard

1 Thread the sausages, ham, peaches, onions and mushrooms alternately on skewers. Place in a single layer in a large baking or shallow dish.

2 Place all marinade ingredients in a large bowl and beat until well combined. Pour marinade over kebabs and leave for 15 minutes to allow flavours to soak into sausages.

3 Remove kebabs from marinade. Cook under a hot grill, brushing occasionally with marinade, until meat and vegetables are cooked and golden brown, about 8–10 minutes. *Note:* If using bamboo or wooden skewers, soak them for a couple of hours in cold water to prevent them from burning during cooking.

Serves 4

P.44-45: The famous ''Puffing Billy'' in Victoria's Dandenong Ranges.

Sausage and Ham Kebabs

Savoury Upside-Down Pie

750 g (1½ lb) minced chicken

1 tspn salt

½ tspn freshly ground black pepper

3 egg yolks

1 cup creamed corn

1 tblspn butter or margarine

1 onion, finely chopped

1 green capsicum (pepper), seeded and finely chopped

1 tblspn chopped fresh parsley

1 tblspn chopped fresh mint

6 rashers bacon, rinds removed

1 sheet frozen ready-rolled puff pastry, thawed

1 Place minced chicken, salt, pepper, egg yolks and corn in a mixing bowl and set aside.

2 Melt butter or margarine in a heavy-based saucepan; add onion and capsicum and fry over moderate heat until onion has softened, about 5 minutes. Add onion mixture and fresh herbs to minced chicken and mix until well combined.

3 Line base and sides of a 20 cm (8 in) round cake tin with rashers of bacon. Spoon chicken mixture into tin; press down firmly and smooth top level. Place sheet of pastry over top and trim edges. Prick pastry with a fork.

4 Bake in a very hot oven 220°C (430°F) for 15 minutes, then lower temperature to hot 200°C (390°F) and bake for a further 30 minutes or until pie is set and pastry is golden brown.

Serves 8

Fidget Pie

500 g (1 lb) shoulder pork

1 tblspn oil or fat

2 medium onions, peeled and chopped

salt and pepper

pinch ground sage, optional

1 tblspn water

2 sheets ready-rolled shortcrust pastry

4 cooking apples, peeled, cored and sliced

1 tblspn chopped parsley

egg or milk for glazing

1 Cut pork into 5 mm (¼ in) pieces and fry gently in oil or fat until lightly browned. Add onions, salt, pepper, sage (if used) and water to pan. Cover and simmer for 20 minutes.

2 Line an 18–20 cm (7–8 in) sandwich tin or springform mould with sheet of pastry and fill with alternate layers of pork, apples and parsley. Cover with remaining sheet of pastry and decorate with pastry trimmings. Make a hole in the centre to allow steam to escape and glaze with egg or milk.

3 Bake in a very hot oven 220°C (430°F) for 20 minutes, then reduce temperature to moderate 180°C (350°F) and bake for a further 30 minutes. This pie can be eaten either hot or cold.

Serves 6

Left: This dingo-proof fence was erected over thousands of kilometres of Outback Australia in the hope of containing the animals. P. 50-51: Rich dairy pastures of Tasmania.

Savoury Upside-Down Pie

Sweet and Sour Pork

500g (1lb) belly pork, rind removed

2 tspn sugar

1 tspn soy sauce

SAUCE

1 small green capsicum (pepper) or ½ cup Chinese pickles

1 onion

¼ cup vinegar

2 tspn brown sugar

salt

2 tblspn tomato sauce (catsup)

2 tspn cornflour

1 cup chicken stock or water

1 tblspn oil

2 slices fresh ginger, chopped finely

1 clove garlic, crushed

Meatball Surprise.

TO COOK

1 egg

½ cup cornflour

oil for frying

1 Cut pork into 2.5 cm (1 in) cubes. Place in a bowl with sugar and soy sauce. Toss well and leave for 5 minutes. Meanwhile, make the sauce.

2 Cut the capsicum or Chinese pickles and onion into 2.5 cm (1 in) squares. Combine vinegar, brown sugar, salt, tomato sauce, cornflour and stock or water in a bowl. Heat oil, add ginger, garlic and prepared vegetables. Saute lightly. Stir in vinegar mixture and bring to the boil. Keep hot while frying pork.

3 Break egg into pork and, with your fingers, toss the egg and pork together. Place cornflour on a sheet of greaseproof paper and toss pork cubes in flour until well coated.

4 Fry pork in enough hot oil to cover until crisp and golden. Drain on absorbent paper. Reheat oil, add pork and cook a further minute. Place on serving dish and pour hot sauce over. Garnish with chopped shallots. The sauce for this dish is also delicious when poured over crisp, fried chicken or fish, and can be varied with chopped pineapple, bamboo shoots, carrots or water chestnuts.

Serves 4

Meatball Surprises

250g (½ lb) small button mushrooms

10 quail eggs

90g (3oz) ham

bunch parsley

500g (1lb) pork and veal mince

1 tspn ground allspice

salt

freshly ground black pepper

1½ cups dry breadcrumbs

oil for deep frying

cranberry jelly, optional

1 Clean mushrooms and cut off tips of stalks; set aside. Place quail eggs in a small saucepan of water; bring to the boil and boil for 3 minutes. Run under cold water, then remove shells; set aside.

2 Finely chop ham and parsley, or mince together in a food processor. Gradually add pork and veal mince and allspice, seasoning to taste with salt and pepper; mix thoroughly.

3 Using wet hands, surround each mushroom and each quail egg with mince mixture, pressing on lightly. Coat balls with breadcrumbs.

4 Heat oil in a deep-fryer; fry balls for 4–6 minutes until brown and crispy. Drain on absorbent paper. Allow to cool, then place in an airtight container or wrap in aluminium foil. Serve with cranberry jelly, if desired.

Makes about 40

Right: Historic Fort Denison in Sydney Harbour forms a backdrop for this twilight fisherman.

Roast Pork with Ginger and Cashew Stuffing

1 leg of pork, about 3½kg (7lb), boned to form a pocket for stuffing

GINGER AND CASHEW STUFFING

2 tblspn butter

¾ cup chopped shallots

1 cup cashews, roughly chopped

1½ tspn grated fresh ginger

grated rind of 1 orange

3 tblspn finely chopped parsley

4 cups fresh white breadcrumbs

2 eggs, lightly beaten

salt and freshly ground pepper to taste

2 tblspn coarse salt

1 For stuffing, melt butter in a frying pan. Add shallots, cashews and ginger, and cook over moderate heat for 3 minutes, stirring. Transfer to a large bowl and stir in the remaining ingredients (except coarse salt).

2 Spoon prepared stuffing into pocket in pork, packing it in firmly.

3 Sew up opening in pork with a trussing needle and fine string, or secure the opening with small metal skewers.

4 Place pork on a rack set in a baking dish. Rub rind all over with coarse salt. Bake in a preheated very hot oven 250°C (475°F) for 20 minutes. Reduce heat to moderate 180°C (350°F) and cook for a further 2 hours or until cooked. (To test whether pork is cooked, run a thin skewer into the thickest part of the meat. The juices should run clear, and the flesh should have no tinge of pink.)

5 Remove pork from oven and allow to rest for 15 minutes before carving. While pork is resting, make gravy from pan drippings, if desired.

6 Remove trussing string or skewers and carve pork crosswise into slices, so that each slice contains some of the delicious stuffing.

Serves 10–12

Right: Roast Pork with Ginger and Cashew Stuffing

Honey-Glazed Ham

4 kg (9 lb) cooked leg ham

½ cup liquid honey

1 cup orange juice

1 tblspn Dijon mustard

2 tspn soy sauce

1 tblspn brown sugar

whole cloves

1 To remove the skin, first cut a scallop pattern through the skin around the shank bone. Starting from the broad end of ham, gently ease skin away from the fat. Continue to peel off gently, and the skin should come off in one piece.

2 Hold ham firmly in one hand and, with a sharp knife, score the fat in a diamond pattern. Be careful to cut just through the fat, and not into the meat.

3 Place ham in a large baking dish. Combine the remaining ingredients (except cloves) in a bowl, and brush about a quarter of the mixture over ham.

4 Stud each diamond in the fat with a whole clove. Place ham in a moderate oven 180°C (350°F) and bake for an hour, brushing every 20 minutes with remaining glaze and drippings in baking dish.

5 If serving hot, allow to rest for 5 minutes, then transfer to a heated platter. If serving cold, ham may be glazed the day before and refrigerated, but allow to stand at room temperature for 20 minutes or so before carving. (Cold meats are more succulent if not served straight from the fridge.)

Serves 20–25

Bacon Muffins

2 rashers bacon, rinds removed

2 cups plain flour

¼ cup sugar

3 tspn baking powder

1 cup milk

¼ cup melted butter

1 egg, beaten lightly

1 Grill or fry the bacon and chop roughly. Grease deep patty tins. Set oven temperature at hot 200°C (400°F). Sift together flour, sugar and baking powder and add chopped bacon. Mix milk, melted butter and egg together with a fork.

2 Make a well in centre of flour. Add milk mixture and stir quickly with a fork, just until dry ingredients are moistened. Do not beat, the batter should be lumpy. Pour enough batter into each patty tin until slightly more than half full. Bake for 20–25 minutes or until golden brown. Serve hot.

You can vary this recipe by adding ½ cup grated Cheddar cheese and ¼ teaspoon cayenne pepper, instead of bacon, to dry ingredients.

Makes 1 dozen

Right: The cotton fields of western New South Wales. P.58-59: Burke Street in the heart of Melbourne is always a hive of activity. P.60-61: The Melbourne skyline over the Yarra River.

Above: Honey-Glazed Ham.

POULTRY TO PLEASE

A few decades ago, poultry was a rarity on our weekly menus, reserved only for special occasions, such as birthdays and Christmas. Today, all that has changed. With new farming techniques Australians can enjoy a wide range of poultry, not just the humble chicken but turkey, duck, quail, spatchcock and pheasant.

The chicken, of course, is a most versatile food source. Its meat can be used in an amazing number of ways from simple roasting to terrines and pates. And the egg is a wonderful little package of nutrition as it is a valuable source of minerals, vitamins and protein and can make a quick and nutritious meal.

Chicken, turkey and duck are rich in niacin, one of the B vitamins, good sources of protein and they also contribute some iron, zinc and other minerals to our diet. If the skin and any visible fat are removed, poultry is low in fat but high in flavour as you will discover with these tempting recipes.

Chicken Paprika

4 chicken breast fillets

1 tblspn olive oil

1 onion, sliced

250g (½lb) small mushrooms, sliced

1 clove garlic, crushed

1 tblspn paprika

1 cup chicken stock

½ cup low fat yoghurt

1 Heat oil in pan, cook onion and mushrooms 5 minutes. Add garlic and paprika, cook 1 minute, remove from pan.

2 Add chicken fillets to pan, cook on both sides until browned.

3 Return onion mixture to pan with chicken stock. Bring to boil, reduce heat, simmer 5 minutes or until chicken is just cooked.

4 Just before serving stir in yoghurt. Reheat without boiling. Serve with noodles.

Serves 4

Mango Chicken

2kg (4lb) chicken pieces

salt

pepper

4 tblspn peanut oil

1 onion, sliced

1 mango, sliced

½ tspn ground coriander

¼ tspn cinnamon

1 cup chicken stock

1 cup cream

½ tblspn flour, mixed with 2 tblspn lemon juice

1 Heat oil and fry chicken pieces, seasoned with salt and pepper. When golden, transfer to flameproof casserole.

2 Fry onion in oil, then combine with chicken in casserole. Fry mango slices in oil, not letting it colour, then add coriander, cinnamon and chicken stock, mix well and bring it to the boil, stirring constantly.

3 Cover dish and cook in 190°C (375°F) oven for approx. 1½ hours, or until chicken is tender. Remove chicken from casserole and keep warm in low oven.

4 Bring mixture in casserole to the boil, then reduce heat to a simmer and stir in the cream and the flour/lemon juice mixture. Cook sauce gently, making sure it does not boil, until it has thickened. Pour over chicken pieces.

Serves 4

Page 62: Soaring above Stanwell Park just south of Sydney. Right: Brisbane's City Hall.

Below: Chicken Paprika.

Chicken Teriyaki Skewers

4 whole chicken breasts, bone removed

8 spring onions (scallions), cut into 1cm (½in) pieces

MUSTARD DIPPING SAUCE

½ cup mayonnaise

⅓ cup Dijon mustard

1 tspn Worcestershire sauce

½ tspn chilli sauce

MARINADE

½ cup sherry

½ cup soy sauce

¼ cup oil

¼ cup dark brown sugar

2 cloves garlic, crushed

freshly ground black pepper

1 Combine dipping sauce ingredients in a bowl. Mix well. Cover, refrigerate 3 hours.

2 Soak 24 short bamboo skewers in water to cover for 3 hours.

3 Combine marinade ingredients in a large bowl, mix well. Cut each chicken breast into 12 equal pieces, giving 48 pieces. Add chicken to marinade, toss to coat. Cover and marinate at room temperature 2 hours.

4 Thread 2 pieces of chicken alternated with a few pieces of spring onion onto skewers. Grill or barbecue on a lightly oiled rack, turning once, about 2 to 3 minutes each side. Serve hot with Mustard Dipping Sauce.

Makes 24

Chicken Galantine Slices

3 double chicken breast fillets

375g (¾lb) chicken mince

200g (6½oz) sausage mince

1 egg, lightly beaten

1 onion, finely chopped

2 cloves garlic, crushed

⅓ cup chopped parsley

9 slices prosciutto

15 pitted prunes

1 Place chicken breasts cut side up on work surface, pound lightly into a rectangular shape with a meat mallet until flattened.

2 Combine chicken mince, sausage mince, egg, onion, garlic, and parsley.

3 Lay prosciutto slices over chicken, place ⅙th of the mince mixture lengthways down the centre of each chicken breast. Place prunes in a row along top of mixture. Top with remaining mixture.

4 Bring chicken up over top of filling, tie at 2cm intervals with string.

5 Wrap rolls individually in greased foil. Place in a baking dish, bake in moderate oven 30 minutes. Remove foil, bake further 15 minutes or until cooked through.

6 Re-wrap rolls in foil, refrigerate until cold. Remove string, cut into slices to serve.

Makes about 45

P.68-69: Sunset over the red dunes near Cordillo Downs in South Australia.

Chicken Galantine Slices

Turkey Hash

2 cups chopped turkey

2 cups diced, boiled potato

1 cup leftover turkey gravy or cream of mushroom soup

2 tblspn finely chopped shallots

salt and freshly ground pepper to taste

4 slices buttered, wholegrain toast

finely chopped parsley to garnish

1 Combine the first 5 ingredients in a saucepan. Stir gently until piping hot.

2 Spoon over hot buttered toast. Sprinkle with parsley.

Serves 4

Quick Turkey Divan

4 slices hot, buttered toast

8 thin slices turkey

375 g (12 oz) can asparagus spears, drained

1 cup cream of asparagus soup

1 cup cream or evaporated milk

salt and freshly ground pepper to taste

3 tblspn freshly grated Parmesan cheese

1 Place toast in a greased, shallow, ovenproof dish just large enough to fit slices. Cover with turkey slices, then asparagus.

2 Combine soup with cream or evaporated milk. Add salt and pepper and pour over asparagus. Sprinkle with grated cheese. Bake in a hot oven 200°C (400°F) until browned and bubbly.

Serves 4

Right: The ruggedly beautiful coastline of South Australia. P. 73: Fortescue Falls in Western Australia. P. 74-75: An old dray rumbles through the rolling hills of the Barossa Valley, South Australia.

Left: Turkey, Quick Turkey Divan, Turkey Creole and Turkey Noodle Bake.

Turkey Creole

1 tblspn rendered ham fat or butter

1 clove garlic, crushed

1 small onion, finely chopped

1 tblspn plain flour

1 tspn Mexican-style chilli powder

½ cup each tomato juice and chicken stock

1½ cups chopped turkey

½ cup sliced button mushrooms

salt

boiled rice to serve

1 Heat ham fat or butter in a medium saucepan and fry garlic and onion until softened. Stir in flour and chilli powder and cook for 1 minute, stirring.

2 Add tomato juice and chicken stock slowly, stirring until the sauce boils and thickens. Stir in turkey, mushrooms and salt to taste. Simmer for 2 minutes. Serve over boiled rice.

Serves 4

Turkey Noodle Bake

3 cups boiled noodles, drained

1 cup chopped turkey

½ cup grated tasty cheese

½ cup chopped celery

2 cups milk

2 eggs

1 tspn paprika or mild curry powder

salt and freshly ground pepper to taste

½ cup breadcrumbs

1 tblspn butter

1 Place a third of the noodles in a greased ovenproof dish. Sprinkle with a third of the turkey, cheese and celery. Repeat with two more layers.

2 Beat milk with eggs, paprika or curry powder and salt and pepper. Pour gently over ingredients in dish. Sprinkle top with breadcrumbs and dot with butter. Bake in a moderate oven 180°C (350°F) for 40 minutes, or until firm.

Serves 6

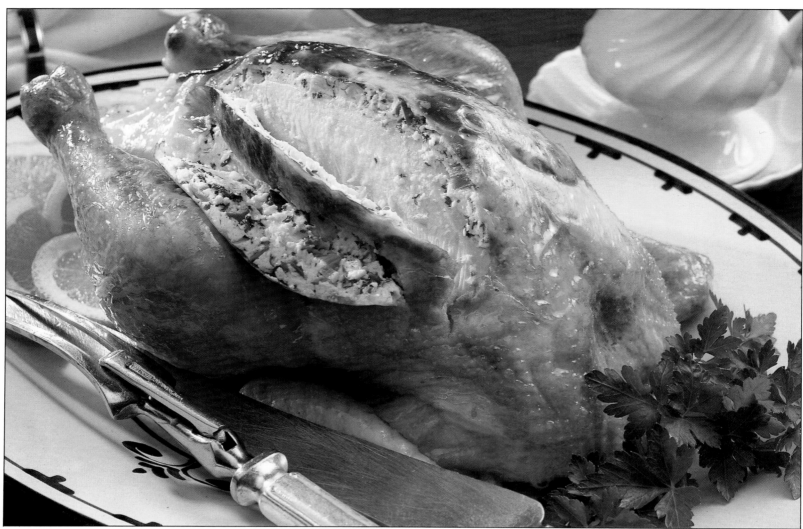

Above: French Roast Chicken with Cream Gravy.

French Roast Chicken with Cream Gravy

size 15 (3lb) chicken

CHEESE MIXTURE

90g (3oz) neufchatel or ricotta cheese

2 tblspn chopped parsley

2 tspn chopped fresh tarragon or ½ tspn dried tarragon leaves

4 shallots, finely chopped

1 tblspn softened butter

salt and freshly ground pepper to taste

STUFFING

2 tblspn butter

1 small onion, finely chopped

2 sticks celery, finely chopped

2 tspn chopped fresh tarragon or ½ tspn dried tarragon leaves

2 tblspn chopped parsley

1 tspn grated lemon rind

2 cups fresh white breadcrumbs

salt and freshly ground pepper to taste

TO COOK CHICKEN

1 cup dry white wine

1 cup chicken stock

1 tblspn butter

FOR GRAVY

1½ cups cooking liquid

extra chicken stock, if necessary

1 tblspn cornflour, mixed with ½ cup cream

salt and freshly ground pepper to taste

1 Remove excess fat from inside of chicken. Combine cheese with the parsley, tarragon, shallots, butter and seasonings.

2 With fingers, gently ease skin away from chicken breast, being careful not to break it. Push cheese mixture evenly over flesh.

3 For stuffing, heat butter in a small saucepan and cook onion until softened. Transfer to a bowl and combine with remaining ingredients. Spoon into cavity of chicken and close cavity with poultry pins.

4 Truss chicken and place, breast-side up, on a wire rack set in a baking dish. Add wine, stock and butter to dish and place in a moderate oven 180°C (350°F). Roast chicken for 1 hour or until skin is crisp and golden, basting frequently with pan juices and turning chicken 2 or 3 times. (Roast breast-side up for the last 15 minutes.)

5 To make gravy, transfer chicken to a dish to rest for 5 minutes before carving. Place baking dish on top of stove and bring liquid in dish to the boil over moderate heat. (If necessary, add extra stock to make 1½ cups.) Stir about a quarter cup of hot liquid into the cornflour/cream mixture, then stir this back into pan. Continue stirring gravy until smooth and thickened, and season with salt and pepper.

6 Remove poultry pins and trussing strings from chicken and carve into 4 portions. Serve on heated plates with a little gravy spooned over. Serve remaining gravy in a sauce boat.

Serves 4

Duck with Orange Sauce

2.5 kg (5 lb) duck

1 orange and 1 lemon

salt and freshly ground pepper

1 small onion, chopped

few stalks of parsley

neck and giblets from duck

2 cups of water

ORANGE SAUCE

3 tblspn sugar

¼ cup vinegar

1 cup reserved duck stock

1 orange

1 tblspn arrowroot

½ cup port

2 tblspn Grand Marnier or Cointreau

salt and freshly ground pepper

2 tspn butter

orange slices and watercress or parsley to garnish

1 Remove excess fat from inside of duck, wipe cavity dry with paper towels. Cut orange and lemon into quarters and place inside cavity. Season duck inside and out with salt and pepper, and truss.

2 Place duck in a deep casserole dish with onion, parsley, roughly chopped neck and giblets, and water. Cover the casserole and cook duck in a moderate oven 180°C (350°F) for 1 hour, turning once or twice.

3 Remove duck, reserving liquid, and place breast-side up on a rack in a baking dish. Return to oven and increase heat to moderately hot 190°C (375°F). Roast duck, uncovered, for 10 minutes, turn breast-side down and roast another 10 minutes. Finally, turn breast-side up and roast another 10 minutes, or until duck is golden brown.

4 Meanwhile, make sauce. Strain liquid from casserole dish and skim as much fat as possible from surface. Reserve one cup. Place sugar and vinegar in a saucepan. Boil for a minute or two until thick and syrupy. Stir in reserved cup of stock.

5 Carefully remove rind from orange with a vegetable peeler and cut into fine strips. Add to saucepan and bring to the simmer. Squeeze juice from orange and mix with arrowroot. Add to sauce and stir until smooth and thickened.

6 Stir in port and Grand Marnier or Cointreau. Heat through but do not boil. Season to taste with salt and pepper. (At this stage, sauce may be taken off heat.) When ready to serve, gently reheat sauce and stir in butter.

7 Remove trussing strings from duck and place on a heated platter. Spoon a little sauce over to glaze and serve the rest separately in a heated sauce dish. Garnish platter with orange slices and watercress or parsley.

Serves 4

Below: The Flinders Ranges in South Australia. Right: A beautiful sunset over a South Australian marina.

Chicken in Black Bean Sauce

500g (1lb) chicken fillets, skinned and boned

1½ tblspn canned black beans

1 tblspn soy sauce

3 tblspn water

1 tspn soft brown sugar

2 tblspn oil

2 cloves garlic, crushed

1 tspn cornflour

1 tblspn water

1 Place chicken fillets in freezer till firm, not frozen. Slice wafer thin.

2 Rinse black beans in water to rid of excess salt. Combine with soy sauce, water and sugar and mash.

3 Cook chicken slices in hot oil in wok or frying pan and stir-fry till chicken changes colour. Add garlic, combine well with chicken and add black bean mixture. Bring to the boil, reduce heat and simmer till chicken is tender, about 4 minutes.

4 Combine cornflour with water and add to chicken, stir and cook till sauce thickens. Serve hot.

Serves 4

Po Chero

8 large Chinese dried mushrooms

4 chicken drumsticks

375g (¾lb) pork fillets, cubed

4 chorizo sausages, cut into 3 pieces

2 tblspn oil

2 onions, sliced

2 cloves garlic, crushed

250g (½lb) orange sweet potato (kumera)

310g (10oz) can chickpeas, drained

2 cups chicken stock

1 tblspn soy sauce

2 tblspn tomato paste

½ cup Chinese cabbage, roughly chopped

1 tblspn cornflour

2 tblspn water

1 Cover mushrooms in boiling water, stand 30 minutes or until tender, drain and cut mushrooms in half.

2 Heal oil in a large frying pan, add chicken and fry until brown, remove. Add sausages to pan, fry until brown.

3 Return all meats to pan. Add mushrooms, onions, garlic, sweet potato and chickpeas. Pour over combined stock, tomato paste and soy sauce, cover and cook on low heat for 30 minutes or until tender.

4 Add cabbage and blended cornflour and water, stir over heat until thickened. Serve hot.

Serves 4

Below: Adelaide is a unique blend of the old and the new. P.80-81: The expansive wheatfields of north-west Victoria. P.82-83: A wild koala enjoys a feed of gum leaves.

Left: Po Chero.

NATURAL GOODNESS

Australia has one of the world's most abundant and varied supplies of fresh fruits and vegetables. And with the range of climates our markets are supplied on a year-round basis with succulent pineapples and avocados, strawberries, capsicums, mushrooms, squash, zucchini to name but a small sample.

Every state has a unique contribution to make to our diet. Tasmania is well-named the Apple Isle because of the wonderful supply of fruit that it sends to the mainland. Victoria has rich market gardens and fine fruit growing areas such as the Goulburn Valley. Queensland, of course, provides us with magnificent tropical fruit and vegetables.

Australia owes a lot to its migrants in that when they arrived they saw an opportunity to grow the fruits and vegetables of their homeland. As a result we include eggplant, okra, snowpeas, pumpkin and pawpaw in our diet as a matter of course.

With this wonderful variety there is no excuse not to include plenty of fruit and vegetables in our diet, which is important because they are the only source of vitamin C. Dark green leafy vegetables, yellow vegetables and orange coloured fruits also contain carotene which is converted to vitamin A in the body plus dietary fibre and some minerals and other vitamins.

P. 84-85: The Wuttagoona Aboriginal caves near Cobar, New South Wales. Left: The rugged wilderness of Oyster Cove in Tasmania.

Soya Bean and Vegetable Loaf

1½ cups vegetable broth

¾ cup finely chopped green capsicum (pepper)

½ cup finely chopped celery

¼ cup sliced mushrooms

¼ cup finely chopped onion

1 garlic clove, crushed

4 cups cooked soya beans

6 eggs, lightly beaten

3 slices wholemeal bread, made into crumbs

1 cup grated carrot

3 tblspn plain flour

3 tblspn finely chopped fresh parsley

½ tspn each ground oregano and thyme

pinch ground cloves

1 In a large saucepan combine stock, capsicum, celery, mushrooms, onion and garlic. Cook for 5 minutes. Cool slightly. Add remaining ingredients, stirring thoroughly to combine.

2 Press mixture into a large loaf tin that has been sprayed with non-stick cooking spray. Bake at 180°C (350°F) for 40 minutes or until golden brown.

Serves 6

Eggs Supreme

2 tspn margarine

1 tblspn finely diced onion

¼ cup finely chopped mushrooms

pinch each salt, pepper and thyme

4 hard-boiled eggs

3 tspn mayonnaise

1½ tspn lemon juice

1 In a small saucepan, over medium–high heat, heat margarine until bubbly and hot. Add onion and saute for 2 minutes. Stir in mushrooms, salt, pepper and thyme and cook 3–5 minutes, stirring occasionally until liquid has evaporated. Cool.

2 Cut each egg in half lengthwise, remove yolks and reserve whites. In a small bowl, using a fork, mash egg yolks. Add mushroom mixture, mayonnaise and lemon juice. Stir to combine. Spoon an eighth of the egg yolk and mushroom mixture into each reserved egg white.

Serves 4

Right: A view from Darling Harbour over to the Sydney city skyline.

Below: Eggs Supreme.

Eggplant (Aubergine) Parmigiana

2 tspn olive oil

1 clove garlic, crushed

½ cup diced onion

½ tspn dried oregano leaves, crushed

1 cup tomato puree

¼ cup chopped fresh Italian parsley

*4 cups sliced eggplant (aubergine),
5 mm (¼ in) thick*

250 g (1½ lb) sliced Mozzarella cheese

100 g (3½ oz) grated Parmesan cheese

1 Heat oil in small saucepan over medium heat. Add onion and garlic. Saute until soft. Stir in oregano and cook 30 seconds.

2 Add tomato puree and bring to boil. Reduce heat to low, cover and simmer for 10 minutes. Set aside.

3 Preheat griller. Lightly spray grilling pan with non-stick cooking spray. Arrange eggplant slices in single layer in pan. Grill 15 minutes or until lightly browned and tender, turning once.

4 Preheat oven to 200°C (400°F). Spoon half of tomato sauce into a 23 cm (9 in) square casserole dish. Arrange half the eggplant slices in pan. Top with half the sliced cheese and half the Parmesan cheese. Repeat layers, using all eggplant and cheeses. Spoon remaining sauce on top. Cover with foil and bake 25 minutes or until hot and bubbly. Let stand 10 minutes before cutting.

Serves 4

Vegetable-Rice Terrine

2 cups cooked brown rice

1 cup vegetable broth

1 tblspn margarine

½ cup diced onion

1 cup sliced zucchini (courgettes)

1 cup sliced mushrooms

1 tspn salad herbs

½ tspn garlic salt

pinch salt and pepper

4 eggs, lightly beaten

6 spinach leaves, stalks removed

6 tspn grated Parmesan cheese

1 In a large bowl, combine rice and broth and set aside.

2 In a large pan, heat margarine until bubbly and hot. Add onion and saute until soft. Stir in zucchini (courgettes), mushrooms, salad herbs, garlic salt and pepper, and cook a further 5 minutes. Remove pan from heat and let vegetables cool slightly.

3 Add vegetable mixture and eggs to rice mixture and stir to combine. Line a 25 x 15 x 4 cm (10 x 6 x 1½ in) ovenproof baking dish with spinach leaves, allowing them to exceed sides of dish. Spoon rice mixture over spinach leaves and, using the back of a wooden spoon, press flat and sprinkle with Parmesan cheese. Fold spinach leaves over rice mixture to enclose. Transfer oblong dish to baking dish, pour hot water into baking dish to a depth of 2.5 cm (1 in). Bake at 180°C (350°F) until set, about 40 minutes.

Serves 4

Right: Windsurfers at Balmoral Beach in Sydney. P.92-93: Some of the fine fare available at the Fremantle markets in Western Australia.

Below: Eggplant Parmigiana.

TUCKER BOX

PIONEER MONUMENT

GUNDAGAI

A TRIBUTE TO OUR PIONEERS.
— UNVEILED BY —
THE RT. HON. J. A. LYONS, P.C.
PRIME MINISTER OF THE
COMMONWEALTH.
28-11-1932.

Above: Peanut Vegetable Loaf.

Peanut and Vegetable Loaf

2 cups fresh wholemeal breadcrumbs

4 sticks celery, finely chopped

¾ cup peanuts, chopped

2 cloves garlic, crushed

1 tblspn Parmesan cheese

2 tblspn chopped parsley

2 eggs, lightly beaten

½ cup tomato juice

1 Combine all ingredients. Spread into a greased and lined 14×20cm (5×8in) loaf pan.

2 Bake in moderate oven for 30 minutes or until set. Turn out, serve sliced.

Serves 6

Left: "Where the dog sits on the tucker box, five miles from Gundagai", New South Wales.

Savoy and Red Cabbage Casserole

3 cups savoy cabbage, coarsely chopped

2 cups red cabbage, shredded

salt

pepper

2 tomatoes, peeled, seeded and chopped

3 bacon rashers, cooked crisp and crumbled

1 tblspn butter

1 cup coarsely chopped onion

1 tblspn butter, extra

1½ tblspn flour

⅓ cup milk

salt

pepper

nutmeg

⅓ cup sour cream

¾ cup grated fresh Cheddar Cheese

1 Spread savoy cabbage in baking dish, cover with red cabbage, season to taste with salt and pepper. Make layer of tomatoes and top with crumbled bacon.

2 Melt butter in frying pan and cook onion, stirring constantly, till it turns golden. Add to baking dish.

3 Melt extra butter in small saucepan, add flour and cook 3 minutes. Add milk and stir till smooth, do not boil. Season to taste with salt, freshly ground black pepper and freshly ground nutmeg. Blend in sour cream and pour over cabbage dish.

4 Spread cheese on top and cover with foil. Bake in 180°C (350°F) oven for 20 minutes. Remove foil and continue baking 30 minutes, or until cabbage is tender and cheese is bubbly and golden.

Serves 4

Grapefruit and Avocado Salad with Bacon

250g (½lb) thick slice bacon, cut into 0.5cm (¼in) strips

2 grapefruit, peeled, reserve rind

2 avocados, each cut into 12 slices lengthwise

juice of ½ lemon

salt

pepper

2 tspn olive oil

2 tspn sugar

⅓ cup Spanish onion, diced

2 tblspn julienned grapefruit rind

1 Blanch bacon in saucepan of simmering water, about 4 minutes. Drain and dry on paper towels.

2 Remove pith and membrane of grapefruit. Remove segments. Toss avocado slices in lemon juice. Remove slices, season with salt, reserve juice. On 4 plates arrange alternate slices of avocado and grapefruit segments.

3 Fry bacon in oil till light brown and crisp, add sugar, reserved juice and season with freshly ground black pepper; heat through.

4 Pour bacon mixture over avocado and grapefruit, add onion. Garnish with julienned grapefruit rind.

Serves 4

Below: The spectacular Wombeyan Caves in New South Wales. P.98-99: A kangaroo and her joey in Queensland.

Right: Warm Cabbage Salad with Walnut Oil.

Haricot Beans and Broccoli Salad

1 cup cooked haricot beans

juice of 1 lemon

¼ cup olive oil

salt

pepper

½ cup thinly sliced Spanish onion

4 cups broccoli flowerets

lemon juice, extra

Spanish onion rings, extra

¼ cup chopped parsley

1 Drain cooked haricot beans and place in salad bowl and toss with combined lemon juice and olive oil while still warm. Season to taste with salt and freshly ground black pepper. Toss in sliced onion.

2 Plunge broccoli flowerets into lightly salted boiling water, return to a boil and cook till broccoli is tender, but still crisp, about 3 or 4 minutes. Drain and refresh under cold running water. Dry gently on paper towels.

3 Add flowerets to beans, toss gently, add more lemon juice to taste and season with salt and pepper. Garnish with onion rings and parsley. Serve at room temperature.

Serves 4

Warm Cabbage Salad with Walnut Oil

4 slices bread

⅓ cup walnut oil

3 bacon rashers, chopped

4 cups finely shredded red cabbage

¼ cup walnuts, roughly chopped

1 Remove crusts from bread, cut into cubes. Heat walnut oil in a frying pan, add bread cubes, cook until golden brown, drain on absorbent paper.

2 Add bacon to remaining oil in pan, stir-fry until crisp. Add cabbage, stir-fry until wilted. Serve sprinkled with bread croutons and walnuts.

Serves 4

Vegetable Stock

2 onions, chopped

2 tblspn oil

4 carrots, chopped

2 sticks celery, chopped

salt

pepper

2 tblspn parsley

1 tspn thyme

1 bay leaf

1 clove garlic, bruised

10 cups water

1 Cook onions in oil till golden. Add carrots and celery and fry 4 minutes. Continue stirring. Season with salt and pepper and 2 tablespoons of the water. Cover pan and cook 5 minutes.

2 Add remaining water, bring to a boil. Skim. Add parsley, thyme, bay leaf and garlic. Reduce heat and simmer till all vegetables are tender. Strain.

Zucchini (Courgette) and Mushroom Vol-au-Vents

30g (1oz) butter

1 onion, chopped

2 cloves garlic, crushed

375g (¾lb) zucchinis, sliced

185g (6oz) mushrooms, sliced

1½ tblspn plain flour

1½ cup milk

½ cup grated tasty cheese

1 tblspn tomato paste

freshly ground black pepper

2 tblspn chopped parsley

½ tspn dried oregano leaves

6×10cm (4in) vol-au-vent cases

1 Melt butter in a saucepan, add onions and garlic, stir over heat until tender. Add zucchini and mushrooms, stir over heat until tender. Add flour, stir over heat for 1 minute.

2 Gradually stir in milk, bring to a boil, stirring constantly. Reduce heat to low, cook 3 minutes. Add cheese, tomato paste, pepper, parsley and oregano, stir until cheese has melted.

3 Heat vol-au-vent cases in a moderate oven for about 10 minutes, pour in hot sauce, serve immediately.

Serves 6

Below: A rare Tasmanian Devil.

Left: Zucchini and Mushroom Vol-au-Vents.

Greek Vegetable Bake

750g (1½lb) ripe tomatoes, peeled and thinly sliced

750g (1½lb) potatoes, peeled and cut into chunks

500g (1lb) onions, cut into quarters

500g (1lb) zucchini (courgette), cut into chunks

2 sticks celery, cut into 3cm (1¼in) pieces

¼ cup finely chopped parsley

2 tblspn finely chopped fresh dill

1 tspn finely chopped fresh marjoram

2 tspn finely chopped garlic

salt

pepper

¼ cup olive oil

1 Spread half the tomatoes in oiled large baking dish. Cover with potatoes, onions, zucchini and celery, all mixed together. Top with remaining tomatoes.

2 Sprinkle with parsley, dill, marjoram, garlic, season to taste with salt and pepper. Drizzle olive oil on top.

3 Bake on top shelf of 200°C (400°F) oven for 30 minutes. Carefully stir vegetables in dish, return to oven and bake 40 minutes or until all vegetables are cooked. Serve hot or in summer at room temperature.

Serves 6

Potatoes Stuffed with Egg and Yoghurt

6 large potatoes

60g (2oz) butter, softened

6 spring onions (scallions), chopped

salt

pepper

6 tblspn yoghurt

6 eggs, beaten

90g (3oz) grated tasty cheese

2 tblspn chopped coriander

1 Bake potatoes in 190°C (375°F) oven till cooked, about 1½ hours.

2 Scoop out inside, mash scooped out potato with butter, spring onion, salt and lots of freshly ground black pepper, the yoghurt and beaten eggs.

3 Stuff into potato shells and sprinkle with grated cheese. Place in oven till puffed and golden. Garnish with coriander and serve hot.

Serves 6

Colcannon

1kg (2lb) potatoes

8 spring onions (scallions), chopped

1 cup milk

60g (2oz) butter

375g (¾lb) cooked cabbage, shredded

salt

pepper

1 Cook potatoes till tender. Drain.

Below: An usual patron of the Silverton Hotel, New South Wales.

2 Place spring onions in saucepan with milk, bring to a boil and add to potatoes. Mash together till mixture is light and fluffy.

3 Melt butter, add cooked cabbage and toss well to coat. Add to mashed potatoes, combine well and season to taste with salt and lots of freshly ground black pepper. Serve hot.

Serves 4

Vegetable Hot Pot

2 cups vegetable stock (see page 101)
1 cup sliced carrot
1 cup frozen beans, thawed
1 cup shredded cabbage
1 cup sliced, flat mushrooms
1 medium tomato, blanched, peeled and chopped
½ cup diced onion
1 tspn chopped, fresh parsley
pinch each salt and pepper

1 In a 3-litre (12-cup) saucepan, combine broth and remaining ingredients. Cook gently until vegetables are tender.

Serves 4

Black, Green and Orange Casserole

500g (1lb) black kidney beans
2 onions, chopped
2 tblspn oil
2 green capsicums (peppers), cut into 2.5cm (1in) cubes
4 carrots, cut into 1cm (½in) slices
2 tblspn chopped dill
425g (13½oz) can tomatoes, chopped
150ml (¼ pint) vegetable stock (see page 101)
salt
pepper
julienne of 1 orange rind

1 Cover beans with cold water, leave to soak overnight. Drain and rinse. Place in pan and cover with water. Do not add salt. Simmer until beans are cooked to your liking.

2 Cook onions in oil till golden. Add capsicum, carrots and beans, cook 5 minutes. Add dill.

3 Add tomatoes with their juice, vegetable stock, season with salt and pepper. Bring to a boil, reduce heat and simmer 25 minutes. Just before serving stir in julienned orange rind. Serve hot.

Serves 6

Above: Camels have served Outback Australians for well over a century. P.104-105: Outback Queensland has some of the largest sheep stations in Australia. P.106-107: Wave Rock in Western Australia. P.108-109: A paddle steamer on the Murray River in South Australia.

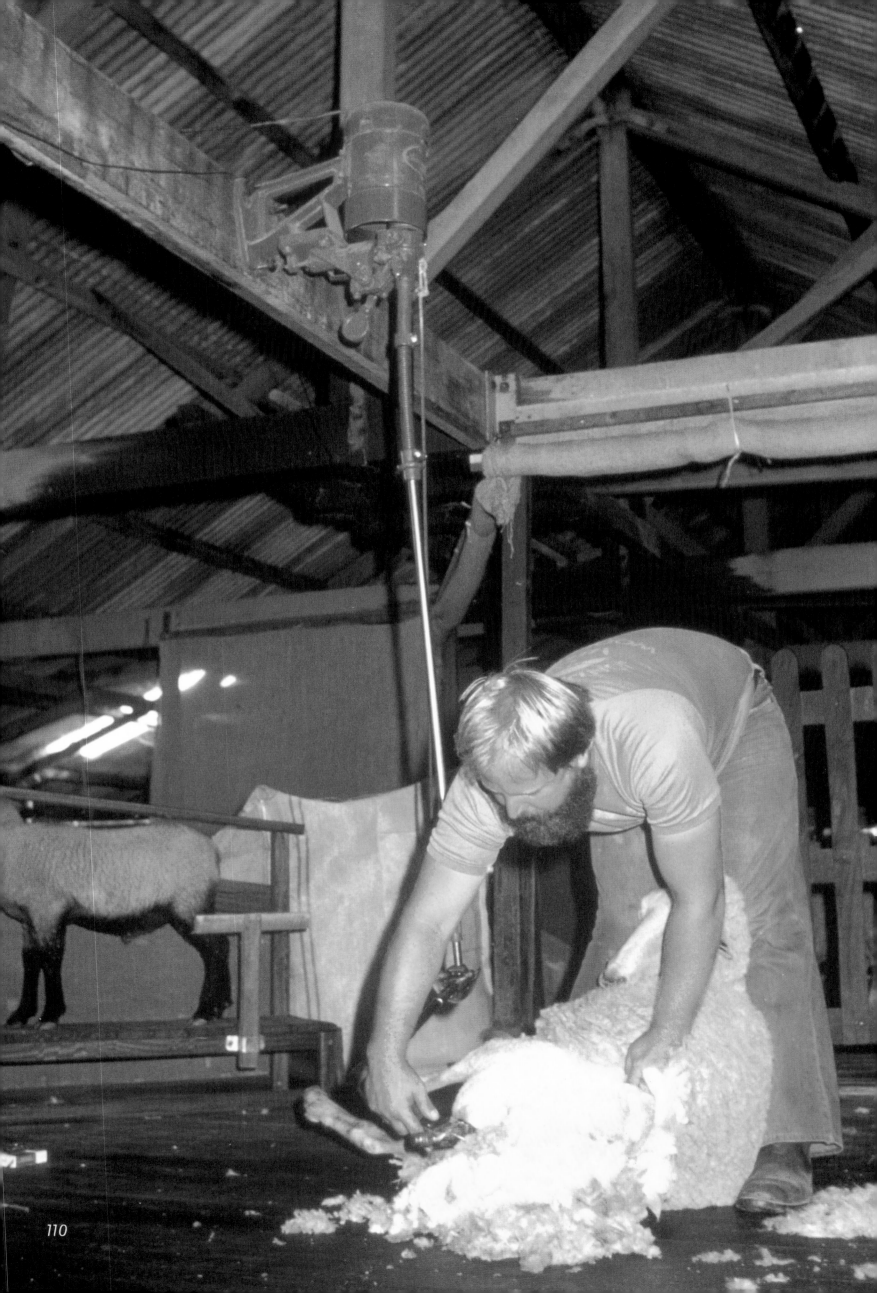

COUNTRY COOKING

In the bush, where a hard day's work is physical, country cooking has traditionally been wholesome and hearty.

Beef and lamb were readily at hand, of course, and all homesteads had their own vegie patch; baked dinners were the order of the day, with roast lamb and baked potatoes and pumpkin being a typical meal.

But there is far more to our country cooking than just plain roasts. The distance from town has always meant that the folk on the land have had to be self-reliant, not being able to pop down to the corner store for a jar of jam, when they ran out.

Consequently, the women of the bush had to produce these goods in their own kitchens and they are rightly proud of their culinary skills, as a visit to any country Show will reveal. Stalls displaying homemade jams, marmalades, chutneys, cakes and biscuits are always thronged and the competition for Best In Show is hotly contested.

Here's a selection of recipes, developed over the years in those country kitchens, that will be enjoyed in any household.

Left: A gun shearer at work in the Jondaryn Woolshed near Toowoomba.

Crusted Pumped Leg of Lamb

2¼ kg (4½ lb) pumped (corned) leg of lamb

water

few parsley stalks

bay leaf

1 tspn black peppercorns

1 tspn whole allspice

1 tblspn each vinegar and brown sugar

3 cups soft breadcrumbs

1 small onion, grated

2 tblspn chopped fresh mint

1 tspn mixed dried herbs

salt and pepper to taste

½ cup drained, crushed pineapple

1 egg, beaten

2 tblspn melted butter

limes, mint jelly and mint sprigs to serve

1 Place lamb in a large saucepan with cold water to cover. Add parsley stalks, bay leaf, the peppercorns, allspice, vinegar and brown sugar. Bring slowly to the boil, then cover saucepan and simmer lamb for 2 hours, or until tender when pierced with a fine skewer.

2 Remove saucepan from heat and allow lamb to cool in the cooking liquid. When cold, remove and pat dry with paper towels.

3 Mix together the breadcrumbs, grated onion, mint, herbs, salt and pepper, pineapple and beaten egg. Brush lamb with melted butter and press crumb mixture on firmly. Place lamb on a rack in a baking dish, and bake in a moderately hot oven 190°C (375°F) for 20-25 minutes, or until crumbs are crisp and golden.

4 Remove lamb to a heated platter. Cut limes in half and scoop out pulp (reserve for another use). Fill lime halves with mint jelly and arrange on platter with sprigs of mint.

Serves 6–8

Right: Adelaide's Festival Hall.

Below: Crusted Pumped Leg of Lamb.

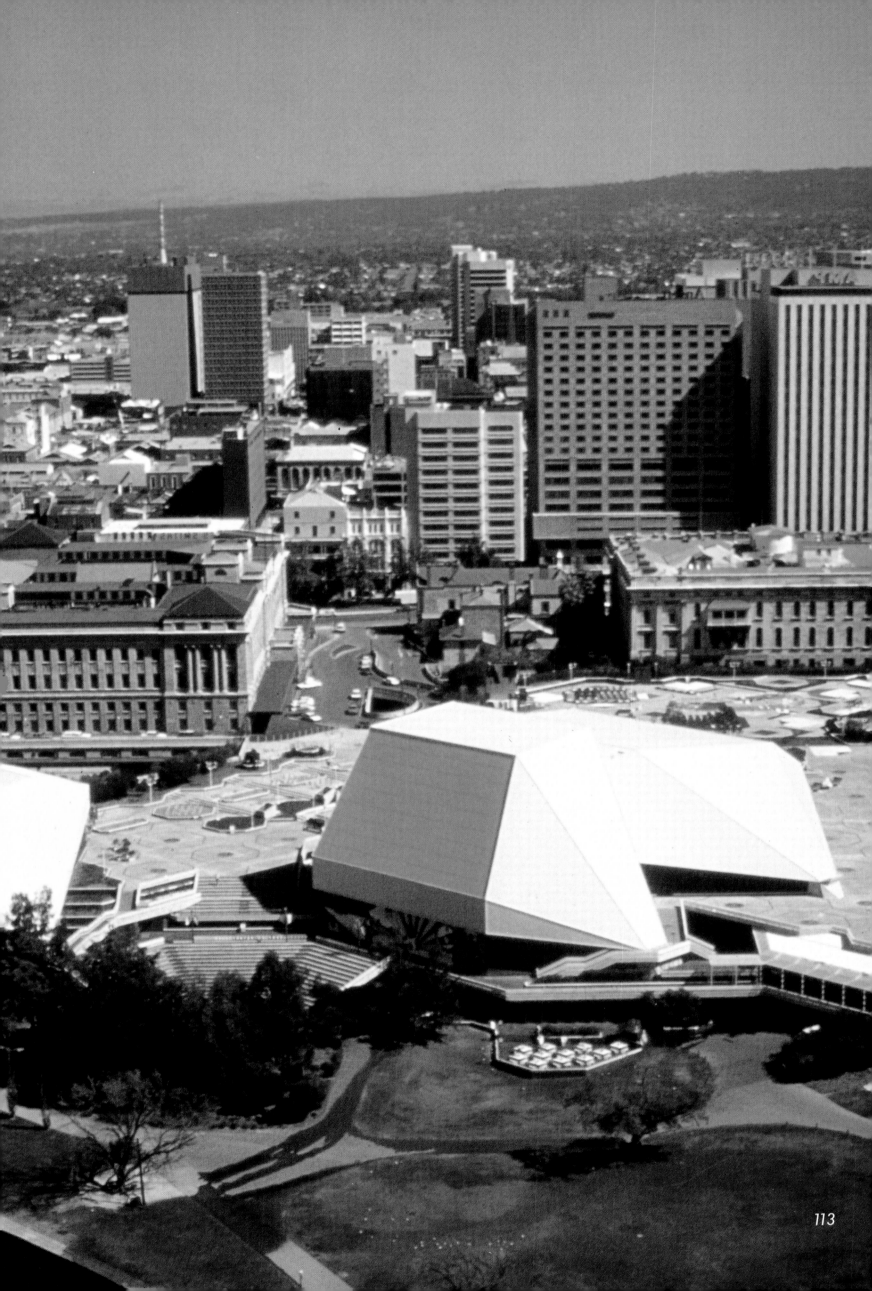

Roast Fillet of Beef with Port and Nut Stuffing

1½kg (3lb) Scotch fillet (rib eye) or eye fillet, in one piece

STUFFING

⅓ cup coarsely chopped pecans

2 tblspn butter, melted

2 tblspn chopped parsley

2 tblspn liquid honey

1 tblspn grated orange peel

¼ cup port

1 egg, beaten

salt and freshly ground pepper

about 2 cups fresh, white breadcrumbs

TO COOK BEEF

1 large carrot, coarsely chopped

3 sticks celery, coarsely chopped

1 large onion, coarsely chopped

2 tblspn butter

GRAVY

1 cup beef stock

½ cup port

salt and freshly ground pepper

watercress to garnish

1 Trim the beef, removing all fat and sinews. Make a lengthwise incision to form a pocket for stuffing, cutting only three-quarters of the way through.

2 Combine all the stuffing ingredients, adding enough breadcrumbs to make a stuffing that is moist, but not wet.

3 Fill pocket with stuffing and tie beef at 5cm (2in) intervals with kitchen string to keep stuffing in place.

4 Scatter carrots, celery and onion in the base of a roasting tin and dot with butter. Place beef on top of vegetables. Roast in a preheated hot oven 200°C (390°F) for 50-60 minutes for medium-rare beef, turning beef halfway through cooking time. Remove beef to a serving platter and cover loosely with foil (it should rest for about 15 minutes before carving).

5 Strain pan juices through a colander into a saucepan, pressing down on vegetables to extract as much liquid as possible. Add beef stock and port to the saucepan and bring to the boil. Boil rapidly until liquid is reduced to thin gravy consistency. Season to taste with salt and pepper.

6 Remove strings from beef. Arrange on a heated platter and spoon a little gravy over the top. Garnish platter with watercress. Carve beef into thick slices and serve remaining gravy separately in a heated sauce boat.

Serves 8–10

Right: Sunlight dapples the magnificent trees in Lawn Hill Gorge, Queensland. P.116-117: The historic Elizabeth Farm homestead in New South Wales.

Below: Roast Fillet of Beef with Port and Nut Stuffing.

Apple Chutney with Sultanas

4 cups vinegar

90g (3oz) pickling spice

1.5kg (3lb) apples, peeled, cored, sliced thickly

500g (1lb) sultanas

½ tspn coriander seeds, crushed

1 tspn black peppercorns, crushed

2 dried red chillies

3 cups brown sugar

2 tspn salt

1 Place vinegar and pickling spice in a saucepan, boil 5 minutes, strain.

2 Combine apples and raisins in a large saucepan, add strained vinegar and bring gently to a boil.

3 Combine crushed coriander and peppercorns in a cheesecloth square together with the dried chillies, tie securely and add to saucepan with brown sugar and salt. Simmer until mixture has thickened. Remove cheesecloth bag.

4 Have ready some sterilized jars, pour in mixture, seal.

Makes 3 x 500g (1lb) jars

Lime Marmalade with Brandy

1 cup lime juice, plus lime peel

4 cups water

4 cups sugar

1½ tblspn brandy

1 Place juice in measuring jug. Separate pith from skin, set pith aside. Cut skin into julienne sticks and add to measuring jug to measure 1 1/3 cups. Add remaining peel to reserved pith.

2 Place pith and peel in a bowl, add 1 cup water. Stand overnight or as long as 24 hours.

3 Place juice and julienned peel in another bowl and add remaining 3 cups water. Stand overnight or as long as 24 hours.

4 Place juice and peel mixture into a large saucepan, strain pith and peel mixture into this, pressing down hard to extract as much flavour as possible. Bring to a vigorous boil, boil 30 minutes or until peel is tender. Measure, add water to give 4 cups. Stand 24 hours.

5 Place mixture in large saucepan, bring to a boil, add sugar all at once, stir until sugar dissolves and mixture boils vigorously. Keep boiling 30 minutes, remove from heat and to test place 1 tablespoon of the mixture on a chilled plate. Return plate to refrigerator and if mixture sets in a few minutes, your marmalade will set. If not, return to heat and test again in 5 minutes.

6 Stir in brandy. Cool marmalade slightly, stirring constantly for 10 minutes. Pour into sterilized jars and seal.

Makes 3 x 1 cup jars

Below: The clear atmosphere of Siding Springs, NSW, is the ideal spot for star gazing.

Left: Apple Chutney with Sultanas.

Apple Chutney

5 green apples, peeled, chopped

2 cups white vinegar

2 cups brown sugar

1 cup sultanas

1 cup raisins

2 onions, chopped

¼ cup chopped glace ginger

2 tblspn yellow mustard seeds

2 cloves garlic, crushed

1 tspn ground allspice

salt

1 Combine all ingredients in a large saucepan, stir over heat until sugar is dissolved. Bring to a boil, reduce heat to low, cook for about 2 hours or until mixture has reduced and thickened, stirring occasionally. Season to taste with salt.

2 Remove from heat, pour into sterilised jars, seal well.

Makes about 4 cups

Apple Suet Pudding

2 cups self-raising flour

1 tspn castor sugar

pinch salt

125 g (4 oz) shredded or finely chopped suet

about 150 ml (¼ pint) warm water

4 Granny Smith apples

3 tblspn sugar

2 tspn plain flour

¼ cup water

2 cloves

1 Sift together flour, sugar and salt in a mixing basin. Toss in the suet and stir in enough warm water to mix a scone-like dough, firm enough to be rolled out. Turn out on a lightly floured surface and knead lightly. Use pastry immediately.

2 Peel, core and slice apples and mix with sugar and flour. Cut off a quarter of pastry for top. Roll out remainder to a large circle and fit to the base and sides of a 1.2-litre (2½-pint) well-greased bowl. Allow any extra pastry to overlap the edge. Fill the bowl right to the top with the sliced apples. Pour in the water and place cloves on top.

3 Roll out the reserved piece of pastry to make a lid, dampen the edges and fit over the top. Press edges well together to seal, and trim away any excess pastry.

4 Cover with greased double-thickness greaseproof paper (fold a pleat across the centre to allow the pastry to rise). Tie securely with string and cover with an extra layer of kitchen foil. It's a good idea to make a string handle over the basin to make the pudding easier to handle while hot.

5 Steam briskly for 2½–3 hours, refilling steamer with boiling water as required. Serve hot with custard, if desired.

Serves 4–6

Below: Precious water is hauled to the surface in the parched land around White Cliffs. Right: Wind and water have eroded these cliffs in NSW to reveal multi-coloured layers of sand.

Rich Ginger Cake

125g (4oz) butter

¾ cup brown sugar

2 cups plain flour

1 tspn ground ginger

pinch salt

2 eggs

1 cup treacle

¾ cup sultanas

3 tblspn milk

½ tspn bicarbonate of soda

1 Grease and flour a deep 15–20cm (6–8in) round cake tin or 23x13cm (9x5in) loaf tin and set oven at moderate 180°C (350°F).

2 Cream butter, add sugar, and continue to beat until light. Sift flour with ground ginger and salt. Beat eggs, one at a time, into creamed butter and sugar, sprinkling each egg with a teaspoon of sifted flour. Stir in treacle, sultanas and remaining flour. Warm milk gently, add soda, and stir into the cake mixture.

3 Turn into prepared cake tin. Bake in preheated oven for 1 hour, then lower heat to moderately slow 160°C (320°F) for a further 30 minutes (if cake is getting too brown on top, cover with a piece of greaseproof paper). Let cool for 5 minutes in tin before turning out.

Serves 6–8

Pineapple Fritters

4-6 rings canned pineapple

plain flour

fritter batter (see recipe)

oil for frying

castor sugar

1 Drain pineapple rings. Pat dry and dredge in flour. Dip in fritter batter. Fry in hot oil until crisp and golden brown.

2 Drain on absorbent paper and serve immediately, sprinkled with caster sugar.

Serves 4–6

Fritter Batter

½ cup self-raising flour

½ cup plain flour

pinch salt

2 tblspn melted butter or oil

150ml (¼ pint) tepid water

1 eggwhite

1 Sift flours and salt into a bowl. Make a well in the centre and pour in melted butter or oil and water. Gradually stir in flour and beat to a smooth batter. Stand for an hour if possible.

2 Beat eggwhite until soft peaks form and stir in very lightly just before using.

Makes about 1 cup

P.122-123: The Swan River in the heart of Perth provides excellent sailing for small yachts.

Rich Cherry Cake

2½ cups plain flour

pinch salt

¼ tspn baking powder

125g (4oz) glace cherries

250g (8oz) butter

1 cup castor sugar

¼ tspn almond essence, optional

3 eggs

4-6 tblspn milk

1 Grease and flour a 23x13cm (9x5in) loaf tin. Set oven at moderate 180°C (350°F).

2 Sift flour, salt and baking powder. Cut the cherries into halves or quarters and toss in 4 tablespoons of the sifted flour until well coated. Cream butter, add sugar and beat until fluffy. Add essence (if used) and beat in eggs, one at a time, with 1 teaspoon of sifted flour (this is to prevent curdling). Fold in the flour alternately with milk.

3 The mixture should be slightly stiffer than plain butter cake. Fold in floured cherries and extra milk if necessary.

4 Spoon into prepared tin and bake in preheated oven for 1½–1¾ hours. To prevent splitting and cracking on top, cover with 2 folds of greaseproof paper for first 30 minutes of baking.

5 Remove cake from oven and stand tin on a wire rack for 5 minutes before turning out.

Serves 8–10

Raspberry Jam

1 kg (2lb) raspberries, hulled

1 kg (2lb) sugar

1 Place raspberries in a large saucepan. Heat slowly until boiling point, stirring constantly. Simmer 5 minutes.

Below: A grim reminder of Australia's history in Port Arthur, Tasmania. Right: Evening fishing on Fraser Island, Queensland.

2 Add sugar and stir over gentle heat until sugar has completely dissolved. Bring to a vigorous boil for 5 minutes, until mixture is about to set. Have ready some sterilized jars, pour in mixture and cover.

Makes 3 x 500g (1lb) jars

Chocolate Crackles

1⅔ cups icing sugar

6 tblspn cocoa

1 cup desiccated coconut

4 cups Rice Bubbles

250g (½lb) copha (vegetable shortening)

1 Combine all dry ingredients in a large bowl. Melt copha over slow heat, allow to cool, then add to other ingredients and mix thoroughly.

2 Place the mixture in paper patty cases and refrigerate until required. These can be made the day before needed.

Makes about 20

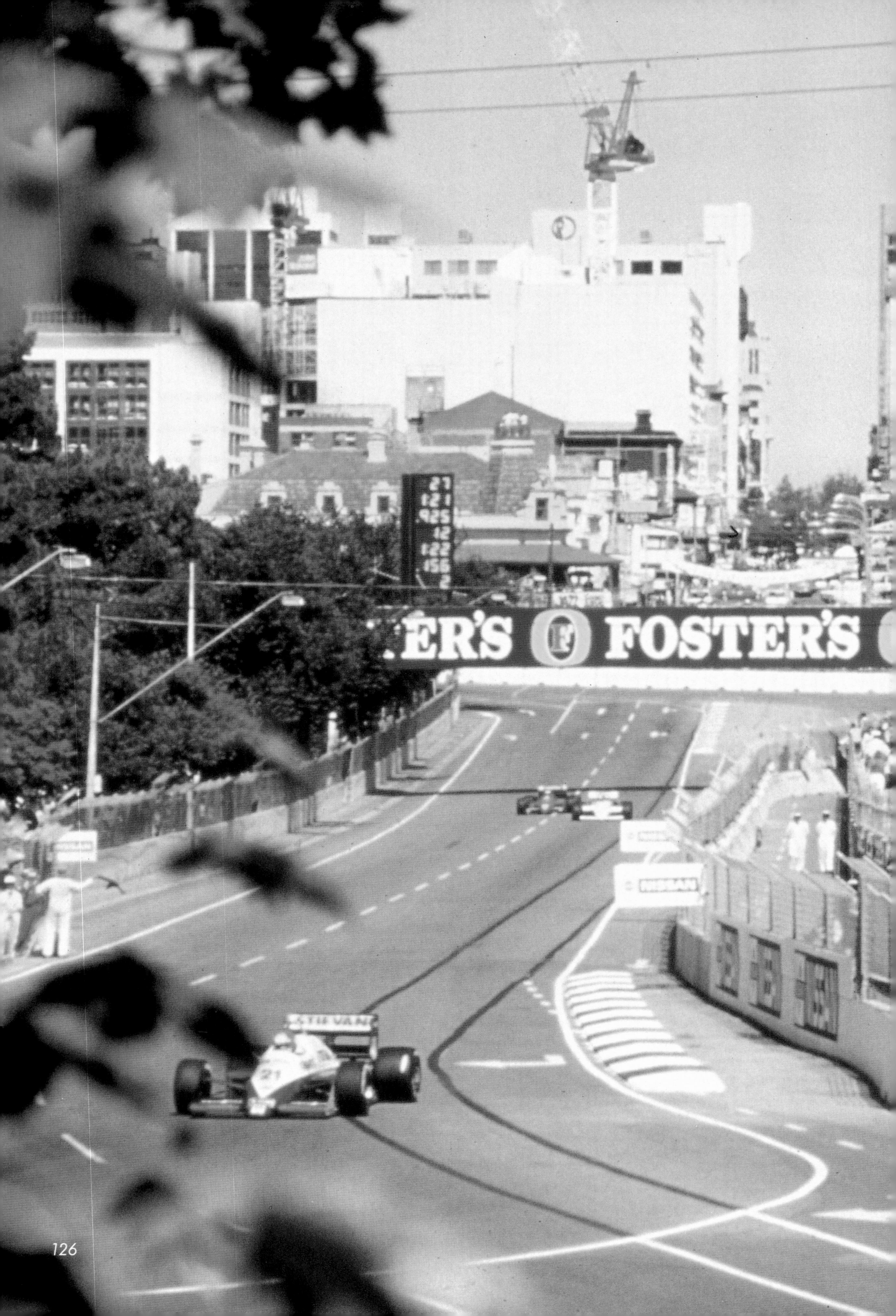
ER'S FOSTER'S
NISSAN

Rough Puff Pastry

2 cups plain flour

pinch salt

185 g (6 oz) butter

150 ml (¼ pint) cold water

1 tspn lemon juice or vinegar

1 Sift the flour and salt into bowl. Rub 30 g (1 oz) of the butter into flour and divide the remaining butter into 2.5 cm (1 in) pieces and add to flour.

2 With a round-ended knife, stir in water and lemon juice or vinegar until the dough begins to cling together. Draw the mixture together gently with the fingers and turn out on a lightly floured board. Shape into a rectangle and roll into a rectangular strip.

3 Mark the pastry into thirds, fold one end up and the other down over it envelope style. Press the ends together to seal. Give the pastry a half-turn clockwise so that the sealed edges are top and bottom. Cover with clear plastic.

4 Repeat the rolling and folding four times more, leaving the pastry to rest for at least 10 minutes between rolling. (If your kitchen is at all warm, put pastry in refrigerator.) This pastry will keep for weeks in your freezer.

Makes about 500 g (1 lb)

Pears Belle Helene

ice-cream

canned pear halves

bottled chocolate sauce

Place a scoop of ice-cream in an individual glass dish. Cover with a pear half and spoon 2 teaspoons chocolate sauce over.

Serves 4

Pavlova

4 eggwhites

1½ cups castor sugar

1 tspn cornflour

1 tspn vinegar

1 tspn vanilla essence

300 ml (½ pint) cream, whipped

1 punnet strawberries or
½ cup passionfruit, sweetened

icing sugar

1 If using gas, set oven at highest temperature just as you start to beat the eggwhites. If using electric, set oven at slow 150°C (300°F).

2 Beat whites at full speed in electric mixer until they stand in peaks. Sift sugar and gradually sprinkle in 1 tablespoon at a time, beating at high speed only until all sugar has been added. Add cornflour together with the last tablespoon of sugar. Fold in vinegar and vanilla.

3 Draw an 18 cm (7 in) circle on greased greaseproof paper or aluminium foil and put on oven slide. Heap eggwhite mixture on the circle on paper. Mould up the sides with spatula and make a slight depression on top. Turn heat to lowest temperature just before putting Pavlova in bottom of oven to cook for 1½ hours.

4 If using an electric oven, cook Pavlova on the lowest rack in preheated slow oven for 45–60 minutes. Then turn off heat and leave Pavlova until oven is cold.

5 Remove Pavlova from gas oven and leave until cold. When cool, spoon whipped cream high in the centre. Arrange three-quarters of the strawberries over cream. Crush remaining strawberries with a fork and push through a sieve. Sweeten with icing sugar. Pour this strawberry glaze over cream and serve.

Serves 8

Left: The Australian Formula One Grand Prix in Adelaide. Above: A crop of safflowers flourish at Muncindi, NSW.

Banana Cake

500g (1lb) ripe bananas, mashed (about 3 large)

45g (1½oz) chopped walnuts

¾ cup sunflower oil

105g (3½oz) sultanas

75g (2½oz) rolled oats

155g (5oz) whole wheat flour

2 tspn baking powder

¼ cup sugar

1 Mix all ingredients together in bowl. Spread into a greased and paper-lined loaf tin.

2 Bake in moderate oven 1 hour or until a skewer inserted into centre comes out clean.

3 Cool 10 minutes before turning onto wire rack to cool completely.

Makes 1 cake

Wholemeal Damper

1 cup wholemeal self-raising flour

1 cup white self-raising flour

1⅓ cups skim milk

1 tspn dry mustard

1 tblspn sesame seeds

1 Sift flours into bowl, return husks from sifter to bowl. Stir in enough skim milk to give a sticky dough. Knead on lightly floured surface until smooth, shape into a round.

2 Place dough onto lightly greased oven tray, press out with fingers to about 3cm (1¼in) thick. Using a sharp knife mark into wedges, cut wedges into dough about 1cm (½in) deep.

3 Sprinkle dough with combined mustard and sesame seeds. Bake in hot oven for 30 minutes, or until golden brown and damper sounds hollow when tapped with fingers.

Makes 1 damper

Fruit and Nut Loaf

1 cup All-Bran

1 cup milk

1 cup wheatgerm

pinch salt

1 tspn bicarbonate of soda

1½ cups mixed dried fruit

½ cup chopped walnuts

1 tblspn honey

1 Set oven to moderately hot 190°C (375°F). Soak All-Bran in milk for 5 minutes. Add wheatgerm, salt and soda, mixed fruit, walnuts and honey. Mix thoroughly.

2 Spoon into 2 greased medium nut-loaf tins and then bake in preheated oven for 35–40 minutes, or bake for 45–50 minutes in a 23x13cm (9x5in) loaf tin.

Makes 2 medium loaves

Right: One of the gracious government buildings in Brisbane. P.130-131: The Blue Lake, Mt Gambier, SA. P.132-133: Mungo National Park, NSW.

Below: Banana Cake.

THE INTERNATIONAL INFLUENCE

Perhaps Australia's greatest asset is its multi-cultural society. We are certainly fortunate to have so many cultures from other lands woven into the fabric of our daily lives.

One of the areas where this colour and diversity is most apparent is our cuisine. As people from different nations have come to Australia, they have brought with them recipes and ingredients that have enriched our cooking. So cosmopolitan is our palate these days that our menus contain a blend of Chinese, Italian, Greek and Thai dishes that we have come to think of as typically Australian.

The Chinese have been influencing our diet since their arrival in the Gold Rush days and it seems that every country town, no matter how small, has at least one Chinese restaurant. After the Second World War migrants from European countries arrived and set up market gardens to grow the kinds of produce they were used to back home. Spaghetti and moussaka were firmly adopted by Australians. In recent years we have benefited from Asian migrants who have brought their herbs and spices and quick cooking techniques to our shores.

Our cuisine has developed under these influences and today we have the finest food in the world. Here is a selection of international dishes that Australians have made their own.

Left: Queensland's tropical fruit and succulent seafood make a delightful buffet.

Chilli Marinated Spareribs

1.5kg (3lb) pork spareribs

1 tspn salt

1 tspn mixed spice

1½ tspn brown sugar

½ tspn chilli powder

2 tspn dry sherry

1 tblspn tomato sauce (catsup)

2 tspns honey

¼ cup stock

1 Slash the rind of the spareribs at 1cm (½in) intervals, cutting through the rind but not through the meat.

2 Mix the salt, mixed spice, sugar, chilli, sherry, tomato sauce (catsup) and honey together.

3 Place the spare ribs in a large shallow dish, pour over the sauce mixture and leave to stand for at least 2 hours, preferably overnight.

4 Using a slotted spoon, remove the pork from the marinade and put the marinade to one side.

5 Place the ribs on a roasting rack and stand over a baking dish containing about 1 cm (½ in) of water. Roast in a moderately hot oven (190ºC) for 1¼ hours or until tender and golden brown. Brush every now and then with the marinade and turn several times.

6 To serve, cut spare ribs into pieces. Pour the remaining marinade into a small saucepan. Add stock, bring to the boil, then lower the heat and simmer for a few minutes. Pour over the pork and serve.

Serves 4–6

Pork Vindaloo

1 kg (2 lb) pork shoulder

MARINADE

4 large onions, finely chopped

4 cloves garlic, crushed

6 tspn garam masala

2 tspn chopped fresh chilli

1 tspn freshly ground black pepper

1 tspn salt

1 cup malt vinegar

1 tblspn brown sugar

1 tblspn ghee or oil

1 Trim excess fat or sinew from pork and cut into 2cm (1 in) cubes.

2 Place all marinade ingredients except ghee or oil in a large glass or china bowl. Add pork and mix until ingredients are well combined. Cover with plastic wrap and refrigerate overnight.

3 Strain marinade liquid from pork and set aside.

4 Heat ghee or oil in a large, heavy-based saucepan, add pork and onion mixture and cook, tossing all the time over high heat until pork changes colour, about 5 minutes.

5 Add reserved marinade liquid and bring to the boil. Lower heat, cover pan with lid and simmer gently for 1 hour.

6 Remove lid and simmer for a further 30 minutes, or until pork is tender.

Serves 6

Below: Australia's unique wombat. Right: Curtain Fig Trees are to be found on the Atherton Tablelands.

Beef and Broccoli Stir-fry

500g (1lb) fillet steak

1 tblspn soy sauce

1 tblspn sherry

2 tspn fresh ginger, grated

1 tblspn oil

½ cup chicken stock

500g (1lb) broccoli, cut into flowerets

2 tpsn cornflour

½ cup chicken stock, extra

2 tspn oyster sauce

2 tspn chilli sauce

1 Cut steak into paper thin slices. Combine in a bowl with soy sauce, sherry and ginger; stand for at least 30 minutes.

2 Heat oil in a frying pan or wok, add steak mixture, stir-fry till brown, remove. Add stock to wok, bring to boil, add broccoli, cover, cook for 5 minutes or until broccoli is tender; drain, reserve stock, transfer broccoli to serving dish, keep warm.

3 Add blended cornflour with extra chicken stock and oyster sauce to pan, bring to boil, add steak strips, stir until heated through. Spoon onto serving dish with broccoli.

Serves 4

Lamb Fillet with Onions

500g (1lb) lamb fillets, thinly sliced

salt

1 tblspn cornflour

¼ cup oil

3 onions, sliced

4 garlic cloves, crushed

2 tblspn sherry

1 tblspn soy sauce

1 Dredge lamb slices in flour, seasoning with salt to taste.

2 Heat oil in frying pan and cook lamb over high heat till golden brown. Set lamb slices aside.

3 In the same pan fry the onions with garlic till soft, add the lamb, sherry and soy sauce and heat through. Serve hot.

Serves 4

Beef Sambal

2 onions, finely chopped

6 chillies, very finely chopped

2 tblspn oil

250g (½lb) topside steak, minced (ground)

salt

1 Cook onions and chillies in hot oil till onion is golden.

2 Add steak and cook till meat is brown.

3 Serve hot with rice.

Serves 4

Right: Lake Burley Griffin, Canberra. P.140-141: The tranquil waters of the Whitsunday's are ideal for watersports such as paraflying.

Below: Beef and Broccoli Stir-fry.

Braised Chicken and Capsicum (Pepper)

500g (1lb) chicken breast fillets

2 tblspn oil

1 red capsicum (pepper), cut into rings

1 green capsicum (pepper), cut into rings

1 onion, cut into eighths

2 cloves garlic, crushed

2 tspn grated fresh ginger

1 tblspn cornflour

1 tblspn sherry

2 tspn soy sauce

1¼ cups chicken stock

1 Cut chicken into strips. Heat oil in a wok or frying pan, add chicken in 2 batches, stir-fry until brown, remove.

2 Add capsicum rings, onion, garlic and ginger, stir fry until tender. Return chicken to pan with combined cornflour, sherry, soy sauce and stock, stir over heat until mixture boils and thickens. Serve hot.

Serves 4

Chinese Fried Chicken

1 size 16 (1.5kg/3lb) chicken

1 tblspn grated ginger

1 tblspn sherry

1 tblspn soy sauce

4 spring onions (scallions), finely chopped

⅓ cup cornflour

½ cup oil

1 tblspn sherry extra

1 tblspn soy sauce extra

2 tspn brown sugar

1 Cut chicken into 8 pieces.

2 Combine ginger, sherry, soy sauce and spring onions and pour over chicken to marinate for 30 minutes, or overnight in the refrigerator. Drain.

3 Dredge chicken pieces in flour and fry in hot oil till golden brown. Discard excess oil, and add extra sherry, soy sauce and sugar to pan. Mix in well. Serve hot.

Serves 4

Apricot Chicken

4 chicken breast fillets

2 tblspn pecan nuts, chopped

1 cup apricot nectar

4 spring onions (scallions), chopped

2 tspn grainy mustard

1 clove garlic, crushed

1 Arrange chicken fillets in lightly oiled shallow ovenproof dish.

2 Toast pecan nuts on oven tray in moderate oven for 5 minutes.

3 Combine apricot nectar with pecan nuts, shallots, mustard and garlic, pour over chicken. Turn chicken to coat all over.

4 Bake in moderate oven for 12 minutes or until just cooked through.

Serves 4

Left: Bush walkers at Wilson's Promontory, Victoria.

Below: Braised Chicken and Capsicum (Pepper).

143

Mongolian Hotpot

1.5kg (3lb) lamb fillets

1 cup canned lotus root, drained and sliced

250g (½lb) Chinese cabbage, shredded

150g (5oz) mushrooms, sliced

1 red capsicum (pepper), sliced

1 green capsicum (pepper), sliced

8 cups chicken broth

2 cups rice, cooked

½ cup spring onions (scallions), chopped

2 tblspn ginger, grated

6 tblspn light soy sauce

3 tblspn hot chilli sauce

1 Slice lamb fillets very thinly and arrange on platter with lotus root, cabbage, mushrooms, red and green capsicum.

2 Bring broth to the boil, place in the middle of the table in a fondue pot, surrounded with the remaining ingredients in separate bowls and let guests help themselves, cooking the meat and vegetables in the broth, then dipping them in the sauces.

3 When all the meat has been eaten in this way, the remaining vegetables can be added to the pot and the resulting soup is eaten.

Serves 6

Pork with Apple Cider Sauce

500g (1lb) pork fillets, all visible fat removed

1 tspn olive oil

1 onion, sliced

2 Granny Smith apples, peeled, cored, sliced

1 cup unsweetened apple cider

1 tblspn pitted prunes, chopped

1 tblspn lemon juice

1 tblspn chopped parsley

1 Heat oil in pan, cook onion and apple for 5 minutes, add lemon juice.

2 Add cider and prunes, bring to boil, simmer for 5 minutes, add lemon juice.

3 Place pork fillets in lightly oiled, shallow ovenproof dish. Pour apple mixture over, bake in moderate oven for 30 minutes or until pork is just cooked, sprinkle with parsley.

4 Serve with sweet potatoes and green vegetables.

Serves 4

Osso Bucco

8 slices veal knuckles for osso bucco

1 tblspn olive oil

2 onions, finely chopped

2 carrots, finely chopped

2 sticks celery, finely chopped

2 cloves garlic, crushed

2 tblspn chopped fresh parsley

½ cup dry white wine

400g (13oz) can peeled tomatoes, undrained

¼ cup tomato paste

1 cup chicken or veal stock

GREMULATA GARNISH:

1 clove garlic, crushed

2 tblspn chopped fresh parsley

1 tspn grated lemon rind

1 Heat oil in pan, brown veal on both sides. Add onions, carrots, celery, garlic and parsley, cook 5 minutes.

2 Add wine and scrape base of pan with wooden spoon. Add tomatoes, tomato paste and stock. Bring to boil, simmer, cook 1 hour.

3 Sprinkle combined Gremolata ingredients over veal, cover, cook 2 minutes before serving.

Serves 4

P.146-147: Sailing is one of the most popular sports in Australia.

Right: Osso Bucco.

Zucchini (Courgette) and Mushroom Pasta Sauce

60g (2oz) butter

2 onions, chopped

425g (13½oz) can tomatoes

2 tblspn tomato paste

125g (4oz) mushrooms, sliced

4 zucchini (courgette), sliced

1 tblspn chopped fresh oregano

2 bay leaves

375g (¾lb) dried pasta, cooked in boiling salted water

2 tblspn grated Parmesan cheese

1 Heat butter in a saucepan, add onion, stir over heat until tender.

2 Add undrained, crushed tomatoes, tomato paste, mushrooms, zucchini, oregano and bay leaves, bring to a boil, cover, reduce heat, simmer 30 minutes or until sauce has reduced and thickened.

3 Serve with pasta, sprinkle with Parmesan cheese.

Serves 4

Rice with Fried Paw-Paw (Papaya)

1 tblspn butter

2 onions, chopped

½ tspn crushed garlic

½ tspn turmeric

1 cup rice

1½ cups tomatoes, peeled, seeded and chopped

1 tblspn finely chopped fresh basil

2 cups chicken stock

salt

pepper

4 slices paw-paw (papaya), peeled, 2.5cm (1in) thick

2 tblspn butter, extra

1 Melt butter in saucepan, add onions, garlic and turmeric. Cook till onions are soft. Add rice, cook 5 minutes, stirring constantly.

2 Add tomatoes, basil, stock, salt and pepper to taste. Bring to a boil, reduce heat to a simmer and cook till rice is soft, but still has a bite. Take off heat, cover and stand till remaining liquid has been absorbed, approx. 30 minutes.

3 Quarter paw-paw slices, remove seeds and fry pieces in butter. Heat through rice, spoon onto heated serving platter, arrange hot paw-paw pieces around and serve.

Serves 4

Below: A monument to Ned Kelly at Glenrowan, Victoria. P.150-151: The lighthouse at Wilson's Promontory, Victoria. P.152-153: The rare quokka, found on Rottnest Island. P.154-155: Adelaide by night. P.156-157: A long red road on a treeless plain in outback NSW.

Right: Zucchini (Courgette) and Mushroom Pasta Sauce.

151

SALADS FOR THE AUSSIE SUMMER

With the wonderful variety of fruit and vegetables available in Australia, we can create an infinite variety of wonderful salads. Crisp and crunchy, with a marvellous blend of taste and textures, salads not only provide us with many of the vitamins and minerals essential for our well-being but are simply delicious as well. They can be served for lunch or dinner and are particularly appetising during the hot summer months.

Salads can be hot or cold, served as a main dish or as an accompaniment. Seafood, pasta and pulses can be combined with salad greens and vegetables to add protein and complex carbohydrates for a well-balanced meal. A good salad dressing is also important. Start with a basic vinaigrette and add mustard, garlic, herbs or even blue cheese for extra zing.

The salads in this chapter are easy-to-prepare, tasty and satisfying. We know you will enjoy them.

Left: Sunshine Plantation, Queensland, where pineapples and passionfruit grow in abundance.

Salad Nicoise

425g (13½oz) can tuna, drained

3 hard-boiled eggs, peeled, quartered

3 tomatoes, peeled, quartered

56g (2¾oz) can anchovies, rinsed

12 black olives

400g (12¾oz) can artichoke hearts

⅓ cup olive oil

2 tblspn taragon vinegar

⅓ cup chopped chives

1 clove garlic, crushed

1 Break tuna into large chunks, arrange into salad bowl with eggs, tomato, anchovies, olives and artichokes.

2 Combine oil, vinegar, chives and garlic in a screwtop jar, shake well, pour over salad to serve.

Serves 6

Potato, Pea and Capsicum (Pepper) Salad

¼ cup mayonnaise

2 tspn lemon juice

2 medium potatoes

1 cup shelled peas, 4 pods reserved

1 red capsicum (pepper), cut into 1cm (½in) dice

4 spring onions (scallions), chopped

lettuce leaves

1 tblspn chopped parsley

1 Combine mayonnaise and lemon juice in bowl.

2 Boil potatoes in skin. Drain. When cool enough to handle, peel and cut into 2cm (¾in) cubes. Combine with mayonnaise in bowl.

3 Plunge peas and reserved pods into very lightly salted boiling water, boil 1 minute, drain, refresh under cold running water. Discard pods. Add peas to potatoes. Add capsicum and spring onions, toss well.

4 Arrange on platter lined with lettuce leaves, scatter with parsley. Serve at room temperature.

Serves 4

Right: Wind-carved sculptures in outback NSW.

Below: Salad Nicoise.

Jerusalem Artichoke Salad with Prawns (Shrimp)

500g (1lb) Jerusalem artichokes

4 spring onions (scallions)

½ cup olive oil

2 tblspn red wine vinegar

salt

pepper

250g (½lb) cooked prawns (shrimp)

2 tblspn parsley, chopped

1 Trim all knobbly bits off artichokes. Cook in boiling salted water till tender, about 15 minutes. Drain. Peel, cut into 0.5cm (¼in) slices. Place in bowl with spring onions.

2 Place oil and vinegar in screwtop jar, season with salt and freshly ground black pepper, shake well to blend. Pour over artichokes. Cover, stand at room temperature for 2 hours.

3 Shell and devein prawns, mix with artichokes and serve scattered with parsley.

Serves 4

Below: Greek Salad.

Warm Broad Bean Salad with Prosciutto

¼ cup olive oil

1 tblspn red wine vinegar

2 tspn lemon juice

2 tspn Dijon mustard

salt

pepper

2 cups freshly shelled broad beans

3 tblspn Spanish onion, chopped

60g (2oz) prosciutto, cut into fine strips

2 tblspn finely chopped parsley

radicchio leaves

1 In screwtop jar combine oil, vinegar, lemon juice and mustard. Shake vigorously till emulsified. Season with salt and freshly ground black pepper. Set aside.

2 Plunge broad beans in lightly salted boiling water, cook till tender. Drain. Pat dry with paper towels.

Right: A crop of sunflowers near Tamworth, NSW. P.164-165: Sydney Opera House by night.

3 Combine with onions, prosciutto and parsley, toss in dressing, check seasoning. Spoon beans onto platter lined with radicchio leaves. Serve warm.

Serves 4

Greek Salad

3 cups shredded lettuce

2 tomatoes, sliced

1 small cucumber, sliced

1 small red capsicum (red pepper), sliced

1 small onion, very thinly sliced

185g (6oz) feta cheese, cut into cubes

12 black olives

⅓ cup olive oil

2 tblspn lemon juice

2 tspn chopped fresh mint

2 tspn chopped fresh marjoram

1 Arrange vegetables, cheese and olives in layers on a large platter or individual salad plates.

2 Combine oil, lemon juice, mint and marjoram in a screwtop jar, shake well. Pour over salad, serve immediately.

Serves 4

Mushroom Salad with Hazelnut Dressing

500g (1lb) firm white mushrooms

juice of ½ lemon

⅓ cup cream, chilled

juice of ½ lemon, extra

2 tspn strong Dijon mustard

salt

pepper

2 tblspn finely chopped parsley

¼ cup hazelnuts, sliced

lettuce leaves

1 Wipe mushrooms with damp towel, trim stems. Slice thinly, place in bowl, squeeze over juice of half a lemon.

2 In chilled bowl thoroughly combine chilled cream, lemon juice, mustard, whisk briskly. Season to taste with salt and freshly ground black pepper, add parsley. Cover and refrigerate.

Below: Victoria's Parliament House, Melbourne.

Left: Pineapple and Avocado Salad.

3 Place hazelnuts in frying pan and saute till the slices start to colour slightly. Cool.

4 Add dressing to mushrooms. Toss well, arrange in bowl lined with lettuce leaves. Scatter with hazelnut slices.

Serves 4

Bean Sprout Salad with Satay Sauce

⅓ cup canned satay sauce

1 tspn sugar

2 tblspn oil

2 tblspn vinegar

salt

pepper

4 cups bean sprouts

⅓ cup coarsely chopped parsley

6 spring onions (scallions), chopped

125g (4oz) white button mushrooms, sliced

½ cup unsalted peanuts

1 In small bowl combine satay sauce, sugar, oil and vinegar till well blended. Season to taste with salt and freshly ground black pepper.

2 In salad bowl combine bean sprouts, parsley, spring onions and mushrooms. Add satay dressing. Mix well. Scatter with peanuts. Toss.

Serves 6

Pineapple and Avocado Salad

1 small pineapple

2 avocados

½ cup mayonnaise

2 tblspn chopped chives

⅛ tspn cayenne pepper

2 tspn grated fresh ginger

¼ tspn paprika

1 Cut pineapple (leaves intact) in half lengthwise. Scoop out flesh, chop roughly, drain on absorbent paper.

2 Cut avocados in half, remove seeds, peel, cut into chunks.

3 Combine mayonnaise, chives, cayenne, ginger and paprika. Spoon pineapple and avocado into pineapple shells, top with mayonnaise mixture.

Serves 6

Fried Potato Salad with Dill Dressing

2 tblspn oil

250g (½lb) baby new potatoes, halved

1 large orange sweet potato, peeled, cut into 2.5cm (1in) cubes

2 sticks celery, chopped

4 spring onions (scallions), finely chopped

½ small red cabbage, finely shredded

DILL DRESSING

½ cup French dressing

1 tblspn chopped parsley

1 tblspn French mustard

1 tblspn chopped dill

1 Heat oil in large pan, add potatoes, cook until potatoes are lightly browned and just tender, drain on absorbent paper.

2 Combine potatoes in bowl with celery and spring onions. Add dressing, toss gently. Arrange salad on bed of shredded red cabbage.

3 To make Dill Dressing combine all ingredients in a jar, shake well. Serve warm or cold.

Serves 4

Lentil and Radish Salad

1 cup lentils, rinsed

½ cup chopped onion

½ cup chopped carrots

1 tblspn chopped parsley

1 clove garlic, crushed

½ tspn thyme, crumbled

1 bay leaf

1 tspn salt

pepper

1 cup radish, thinly sliced

⅓ cup parsley, chopped, extra

2 tblspn chopped chives

¾ cup vinaigrette

lettuce leaves

1 In saucepan combine lentils, onions, carrot, parsley, garlic, thyme and bay leaf. Add 4 cups water, salt and pepper to taste, bring to a boil, cover and simmer about 20 minutes or until lentils are just tender. Drain. Discard bay leaf. Place lentils in bowl, cover and stand 20 minutes to cool.

2 Add radish, parsley and chives, toss with vinaigrette. Line platter with lettuce leaves, arrange lentil salad on top. Serve at room temperature.

Serves 4

Left: The old Ferrier woolpress in ''Kinchega'' woolshed, which is now part of the Kinchega National Park. P.170-171: A typical farmhouse nestled in the rolling hills of south-west Western Australia.

Below: Fried Potato Salad with Dill Dressing.

Chicken Salad with Thyme Dressing

2 Spanish onions

6 chicken breast fillets

2 tblspn oil

salt

2 tblspn red wine vinegar

1 tblspn fresh thyme leaves

2 tblspn oil, extra

1 small mignonette lettuce

½ bunch endive

1 Cut onions into paper-thin slices. Cut chicken into strips.

2 Heat oil in a frying pan, add half the chicken, stir-fry until just cooked, remove, repeat with remaining chicken, remove. Season to taste with salt.

3 Add vinegar to pan, stir into pan juices, strain. Combine vinegar mixture in a screwtop jar with thyme and extra oil, shake well.

4 Arrange mignonette and endive on a serving plate. Top with chicken strips and onion rings. Pour over thyme dressing just before serving.

Serves 8

Julienne Salad of Leek, Zucchini (Courgette) and Beetroot

3 leeks, cleaned of all grit

3 zucchini (courgette)

4 medium sized beetroot

1 lettuce, shredded

½ red cabbage, finely shredded

DILL DRESSING:

juice of 1 lemon

1 tblsp dill

1 tspn sugar

¼ tspn salt

freshly ground black pepper

⅓ cup olive oil

1 Simmer whole cleaned leeks in water to cover until tender, about 12 minutes. Drain and cool. Cut into julienne sticks.

2 Cook zucchini in boiling water to cover until tender, about 30 minutes. Drain and cool. Cut into julienne sticks.

3 Cook beetroot in gently boiling water to cover until tender, about 30 minutes. Drain and cool, cut into julienne sticks.

4 On a large platter make rings, beginning from the outside edge, of lettuce, red cabbage, leek, beetroot and zucchini in the middle.

5 Combine all dressing ingredients in a screwtop jar, shake well and drizzle over the salad.

Serves 4

Below: The tranquil waters of Batemans Bay, NSW.

Right: Chicken Salad with Thyme Dressing.

Mushroom and Radish Salad with Curry Dressing

1 cup sour cream

1 tblspn freshly squeezed lemon juice

1 tblspn olive oil

2 tspn curry powder

salt

pepper

1 bunch radish, thinly sliced

250g (½lb) button mushrooms, thinly sliced

4 spring onions (scallions), cut into 0.5cm (¼in) pieces

1 Combine sour cream, lemon juice, olive oil and curry powder in a bowl. Whisk briskly until dressing is smooth. Season to taste with salt and freshly ground black pepper.

2 Place radish and mushrooms in a salad bowl, add spring onions and very gently fold in curry dressing.

Serves 4

Snowpea Salad with Pinenuts

2 tblspn pinenuts

1 tblspn white wine vinegar

1½ tblspn chopped fresh basil

freshly ground black pepper

⅓ cup olive oil

1 red capsicum (pepper), julienned

375g (¾lb) snowpeas

1 Place pinenuts on baking tray and roast in 200°C (400°F) oven 10 minutes or until light golden. Remove and set aside.

2 Combine vinegar, basil, pepper and oil in a screwtop jar, shake until mixture emulsifies.

3 Plunge capsicum strips into lightly salted boiling water, cook 20 seconds, drain and add to vinaigrette.

■ *Above: The city of Hobart.*

4 Plunge snowpeas into salted boiling water, let water return to the boil and drain immediately. Refresh under cold running water. Drain and pat dry.

5 Remove capsicum strips from vinaigrette, arrange attractively on plates with snowpeas, drizzle with vinaigrette and scatter with pinenuts.

Chilli Broccoli Salad

1kg (2lb) broccoli

salt

pepper

1 red chilli, seeds removed, sliced into rings

DRESSING

⅓ cup olive oil

2 tblspn white wine vinegar

1 tblspn light soy sauce

2 tspn Dijon mustard

⅛ tspn chilli flakes

1 Separate broccoli stems and heads. Divide heads into flowerets about 2.5cm (1in) across. Peel stems and slice thinly diagonally.

2 Plunge broccoli into salted boiling water until just tender but still crisp, about 3 minutes. Drain and refresh under cold running water, drain thoroughly. Season with salt and freshly ground black pepper. Place in salad bowl, cover and chill in refrigerator.

3 To make dressing combine oil, vinegar, soy sauce, mustard and chilli flakes in screwtop jar. Shake to blend well.

4 Drizzle broccoli with dressing, toss gently and scatter with chilli rings. Serve immediately once the salad has been dressed or it will lose its lovely bright colour.

Serves 6

Witlof Salad with Walnuts

500g (1lb) witlof

¼ cup chopped walnuts

2 hard-boiled eggs

½ cup Parmesan cheese slivers

DRESSING

3 tblspn walnut oil

2 tspn white vinegar

2 tspn lemon juice

2 spring onions (scallions), chopped

salt

pepper

1 Separate witlof leaves, if necessary wipe clean with damp cloth.

2 Place walnuts on oventray and roast in moderate oven 15 minutes, until walnuts are golden and crisp. Cool and set aside.

3 Mash egg yolks with fork and cut whites into thin strips.

4 Place all dressing ingredients in a screwtop jar, shake well to blend.

5 To assemble the salad arrange witlof leaves in a shallow salad bowl. Scatter with walnuts, egg yolk crumbs, egg white strips and the cheese slivers. Drizzle with dressing.

Serves 4

Below: The Mt Prior winery in Rutherglen, Victoria.
P.176-177: A spectacular view of the Parkes telescope in New South Wales. P.178-179: The Lady Stelfox cruises the Tamar River near Launceston.
P.180-181: A desert specialist, the Boab tree, Western Australia.

BEAUTIFUL BAKING

The rolling wheat fields of Australia produce some of the best grain in the world. Consequently, our flour is fresh and wholesome. Whether you use white or wholemeal flour, you can be sure that your baking will be the best. And who can resist freshly baked breads and cakes?

Fresh from the oven, bread or rolls can turn an ordinary meal into a memorable one and homemade cakes and biscuits are not only cheaper than store-bought versions, but are tastier and more nutritious.

Baking is a skill that is easily learned, if you follow some basic rules. Unlike general cooking where a dash of this or a dollop of that can produce a splendid result, you have to measure ingredients accurately for baking as success depends on everything being in proper proportion.

Follow the recipes in this chapter and you will have success with results that will please the whole family.

Left: Harvest time in Horsham, Victoria.

Chocolate Pecan Brownies

1½ cups pecan nuts

½ cup plain flour

¼ cup sugar

½ cup dark corn syrup

90g (3oz) dark chocolate, chopped

45g (1½oz) butter

2 eggs, lightly beaten

1 tblspn rum

1 tblspn icing sugar

1 Chop pecans finely by hand (a food processor is unsuitable). Combine pecans and sifted flour in a bowl.

2 Combine sugar and corn syrup in a saucepan, stir over heat until boiling. Remove from heat, add chocolate and butter, stir until chocolate has melted and mixture is smooth. Add eggs and rum, stir until combined.

3 Add this mixture to the flour and pecans, stir until combined.

4 Grease a 19cm x 29cm (7½in x 11½in) lamington pan, line base and sides with paper, grease paper. Spread mixture evenly into pan. Bake in moderate oven for about 30 minutes or until set. Cool in pan 10 minutes before turning onto wire rack to cool.

5 Dust with sifted icing sugar, cut into small squares.

Makes 24 squares

Hazelnut Bread

3 eggwhites

½ cup castor sugar

1 cup plain flour

150g (5oz) roasted hazelnuts

1 Beat eggwhites in a small bowl with electric mixer until soft peaks form. Gradually add sugar 1 tablespoon at a time, beat until dissolved between additions.

2 Fold in flour and hazelnuts, spread evenly into a greased and lined bar pan 7cm x 25cm (2¾in x 10in).

3 Bake in moderate oven 30 minutes or until light golden brown. Turn onto wire rack to cool. Wrap in foil, stand overnight.

4 Using an electric knife or very sharp knife, slice loaf thinly. Bake slices on an oven tray in a slow oven for 45 minutes or until dry and crisp. Store in airtight container for up to 1 month.

Makes about 48 slices

Walnut Loaf

1 cup unsalted butter, room temperature

1¼ cups sugar

4 eggs, room temperature

1 tblspn kirsch

2¼ cups sifted plain flour

1½ tspn baking powder

110g (3½oz) finely ground walnuts

confectioners' sugar

1 Place butter in a processor. Beat until soft and creamy. Add sugar gradually, thoroughly incorporating one lot before adding the next. Add eggs, one at a time, blending well after each addition. Add kirsch.

2 Add combined flour and baking powder. Mix in lightly. Add walnuts, combine well. Pour into a greased loaf pan, smooth top.

3 Place in lower half of a 190°C (375°F) oven, bake 1 hour, or until cake is done when tested.

4 Cool in the loaf pan 10 minutes, unmould onto a wire rack to cool completely. Cut into slices, serve sprinkled lightly with confectioners' sugar.

Serves 12

P.187: Victoria's Russell Falls.
P.188-189: Tending the flock.

Right: Chocolate Pecan Brownies.

Spiced Apple Wholemeal Cake

2 apples, peeled, cored and sliced

¾ cup water

125g (4oz) butter

1 cup raw sugar

2 eggs

1 cup wholemeal plain flour

1 cup self-raising flour

½ tspn bicarbonate of soda

1 tspn mixed spice

¼ cup walnuts, chopped

½ cup raisins, chopped

¾ cup whipping cream

sifted icing sugar for decoration

1 Grease and line a 23cm (9in) round cake pan.

2 Cook apples in water until tender, remove from heat, puree or sieve until smooth, cool.

3 Cream butter and sugar in small bowl with electric mixer until light and fluffy. Add eggs, beat until combined.

Below: Spiced Apple Wholemeal Cake.

4 Add half the sifted dry ingredients and half the apple mixture, beat on very low speed until just combined. Add remaining dry ingredients and apple mixture, beat until combined. Stir in walnuts and raisins.

5 Spread mixture evenly into prepared pan. Bake in moderate oven for 40 minutes or until golden brown. Turn onto wire racks to cool. When cold split cake in half, fill with cream, dust with icing sugar.

Bavarian Apple Cake

½ cup butter, softened

1 cup sugar

2 eggs

1 cup flour

1 tspn baking powder

1 tspn vanilla

⅓ cup sugar

1 tspn cinnamon

4 large apples, peeled, and cored

1 Beat butter, sugar and eggs. Add flour, baking powder and vanilla. Mix in well. Pour into 20 x 20cm (8 x 8in) baking dish.

2 Slice apples thinly and combine with sugar to taste and cinnamon. Arrange slices prettily on top of cake batter and press in lightly. Bake 1 hour in 180°C (350°F) oven or till done when tested. Cool. To serve cut into squares.

Pear Bread

375g (12oz) self-raising flour

½ tspn salt

90g (3oz) castor sugar

155g (5oz) dried pears, soaked *overnight*, drained and chopped

2 tblspn pistachio nuts, *coarsely* chopped

1 tspn grated lemon rind

2 eggs

¾ cup milk

¼ cup melted butter

1 Sift flour with salt, add sugar and pears, pistachios and lemon rind. Mix well.

2 Beat eggs, add milk. Add flour mixture to egg and milk and combine well. Add melted butter.

3 Pour into greased loaf tin and bake in 180°C (350°F) oven for 1¼ hours or until done when tested.

Lemon and Pecan Loaf

1½ cups plain flour

¾ cup self-raising flour

180g (6oz) butter

1 cup castor sugar

1 tblspn grated lemon rind

½ cup chopped pecan nuts

3 eggs

¾ cup milk

⅓ cup lemon juice

2 tblspn sugar

1 Grease and line a 20 x 14cm (8 x 5½in) loaf pan.

2 Sift flours into a bowl, rub in the butter. Stir in sugar, lemon rind and pecans.

3 Combine lightly beaten eggs and milk, add to mixture all at once, stir until combined.

3 Pour into prepared pan, bake in moderately slow oven for 1 hour or until golden brown and cooked through. Turn onto wire rack.

5 Heat lemon juice and sugar in a small suacepan until sugar is dissolved, spoon over hot cake.

Dutch Spice Cake

125g (4oz) butter

1½ cups dark brown sugar

4 eggs, beaten

½ cup milk

315g (10oz) plain flour

1 tspn salt

1½ tspn baking soda

2 tspn cinnamon

¼ tspn cloves

¼ tspn nutmeg

1 Cream butter, add sugar, beat till light and fluffy. Add eggs and milk, combine well.

Right: Sturt's Desert Pea, South Australia's floral emblem.

Left: Lemon and Pecan Loaf.

2 Combine flour, salt, baking soda, cinnamon, cloves and nutmeg. Add to butter mixture, mix in thoroughly.

3 Bake in 180°C (350°F) oven for 1 hour or until done when tested. Turn out and cool.

Cheese and Herb Bread

1½ cups milk

¼ cup sugar

1 tblspn salt

3 tspn mixed herbs

125g (4oz) grated Cheddar cheese

2 sachets active dry yeast

¼ cup butter

2 eggs

8 cups plain flour

1 Scald the milk. Then add the sugar, salt, mixed herbs and grated cheese. Stir until cheese melts and sugar and salt are dissolved. Allow to become luke warm, about 35°C (95°F).

2 Place ½ cup warm 45°C (110°F) water in a bowl and sprinkle over the yeast, stirring to dissolve.

3 Place the yeast, milk, butter, eggs and half the flour in a bowl and beat until well combined. Start adding the rest of the flour, mixing in well. The dough should leave the sides of the bowl.

4 Knead for about 10 minutes on a lightly floured board. Then place the dough in a greased bowl, turning once to coat the dough, cover and leave in a draught-free spot for about one hour or until doubled in bulk.

5 Turn out the dough, form into two loaves and place in greased pans 23 x 12 x 8cm (9 x 5 x 3in). Cover and let rise until doubled, about one hour.

6 Bake in a preheated 200°C (400°F) oven for about 40 minutes, watch that the bread doesn't brown too quickly. Cover with foil if the loaves are getting too dark on top. turn out on to wire racks to cool.

Makes 2 loaves

Cheesy Wholemeal Parathas

3 cups plain flour

1 cup wholemeal plain flour

60g (2oz) butter

1½ cup water

1 cup mashed potato

1 cup grated Cheddar cheese

2 tspn curry powder

1 tspn ground cumin

90g (3oz) butter, extra

1 Combine flours in a bowl, rub in butter. Stir in water, stir until combined. Turn onto lightly floured surface, knead until smooth, about 5 minutes, stand 5 minutes.

2 Divide mixture into 12 portions, press each out to form a circle. Combine potato, cheese, curry and cumin, divide evenly over circles. Press edges of circles firmly together to enclose filling, roll carefully into a 10cm (4in) circle.

3 Melt extra butter in a frying pan, cook parathas in 3 batches, cooking on either side until golden brown and cooked through; add extra butter if necessary.

Makes 12

Gingerbread

125g (4oz) butter

1 cup golden syrup

90g (3oz) sugar

1 tblspn marmalade

½ cup milk

125g (4oz) self-raising flour

salt

1 tspn ground ginger

1 tspn mixed spice

½ tspn bicarbonate of soda

125g (4oz) wholemeal flour

2 eggs

1 Place butter, syrup, sugar, marmalade and milk in a saucepan and heat until sugar dissolves.

2 Sift self-raising flour with a pinch of salt, ginger and mixed spice. Add the bicarbonate of soda and then stir in wholemeal flour. Combine this mixture with the butter and sugar mixture.

3 Beat in the eggs and beat well until batter is smooth. Pour into a greased 20cm (8in) square cake pan and bake in 160°C (325°F) oven for about 1½ hours or until the centre of the cake springs back when pressed with a finger. Cut into squares to serve.

Blueberry Cake

250g (½lb) butter

250g (½lb) sugar

4 eggs

250g (½lb) plain flour

¼ tspn salt

1 tblspn ground almonds

juice of 1 lemon

250g (½lb) blueberries, rinsed

¼ cup sugar, extra

¼ cup almonds, slivered

1 Cream butter, add sugar and beat till fluffy. Add eggs, combine well. Add flour and salt a quarter at a time. Incorporate thoroughly. Stir in ground almonds and lemon juice.

2 Pour half into buttered baking dish. Add blueberries and sprinkle with sugar to taste. Top with remaining cake mixture. Sprinkle with slivered almonds. Cook in 180°C (350°F) oven for 1 hour or until done when tested.

Left: The Brolga of Queensland. P.194-195: Mining in the Pilbara, Western Australia.

Below: Cheesy Wholemeal Parathas.

194

Spring Blossom Cake

SPONGE

4 eggs, separated

1 cup castor sugar

1½ cups self-raising flour

pinch salt

1 tspn butter or margarine, melted

⅓ cup boiling water

FILLING

125g (4oz) cream cheese

60g (2oz) unsalted butter or margarine

¾ cup icing sugar, sifted

2 tblspn mandarin liqueur or almond essence to taste

1 tblspn finely chopped mixed peel

310g (10oz) can mandarin segments, drained

Below: The Buchan caves in East Gippsland, Victoria.

Right: Spring Blossom Cake.

ICING

¾ cup icing sugar

1 tspn coffee powder

1 tspn butter or margarine

1-2 tblspn hot water

TO DECORATE

whipped cream

shreds of mandarin peel

1 Set oven to 190°C (375°F). Grease two 20cm (8in) sandwich tins and dust lightly with flour. Beat eggwhites until stiff peaks form, add sugar gradually and beat until thick and shiny. Add egg yolks one at a time, beating until well combined.

2 Sift flour and salt together 3 times and fold gently through the egg mixture.

3 Mix butter and boiling water together. Pour around the edge of the mixture and fold in gently. Pour the mixture into the prepared tins.

4 Bake in preheated oven for 20–25 minutes or until sponge is firm to touch. Remove from oven and sit on a wet tea-towel (this helps to release the cake without damage) for 2 minutes, then turn out onto a wire rack to cool. Place one half of sponge on a serving plate.

5 Beat together the cream cheese, butter, icing sugar and liqueur until creamy and well combined. Stir in mixed peel. Spread half the mixture over the sponge cake then top with mandarin segments, reserving some for decoration. Spread the remaining cheese mixture over and top with the other half of sponge.

6 To make the icing: Sift icing sugar into a bowl. Add coffee powder and butter and beat in the hot water until mixture is smooth. Spoon onto cake and spread over the top of cake. Allow to set. Decorate with rosettes of whipped cream, reserved mandarin segments and shreds.

Above: Rich Chocolate Cake.

Pumpkin Bread

1 cup sugar

220g (7oz) pumpkin, cooked and mashed

1 small egg

¼ cup oil

1¼ cups plain flour

1 tspn baking powder

½ tspn cinnamon

¼ tspn ground cloves

¼ tspn salt

½ cup dates, roughly chopped

½ cup walnuts, coarsely chopped

1 Combine sugar, pumpkin and egg in bowl and beat till smooth. Add oil, mix well.

2 Add flour, baking powder, cinnamon, cloves and salt. Combine thoroughly. Add dates and nuts. Mix in well.

3 Pour into greased loaf pan and bake in 180°C (350°F) oven for 1 hour, or until done when tested. Turn out and cool.

Rich Chocolate Cake

CAKE

1 tblspn vinegar

1 cup milk

1½ cups plain flour

pinch salt

½ cup cocoa

1½ tspn bicarbonate of soda

1¼ cups castor sugar

185g (6oz) butter or margarine, melted and cooled

1 tspn vanilla essence

2 eggs, lightly beaten

FILLING

1 cup thickened cream, lightly whipped

1 cup fanned strawberries

TO DECORATE

extra whipped cream

extra fanned strawberries

1 Add vinegar to milk, stir and set aside.

2 Sift flour, salt, cocoa, bicarbonate of soda and sugar into a bowl. Pour in the melted butter and half the soured milk and beat well for 2 minutes. Add vanilla essence, the remaining soured milk and eggs and beat for another 2 minutes.

3 Pour mixture into 2 greased 23 cm (9 in) sandwich tins that have been base lined with greased greaseproof paper. Bake at 180°C (350°F) for 30–35 minutes or until a skewer inserted in the centre comes out clean. Allow to cool in the tins for 5 minutes then turn out onto a wire rack to cool.

4 When cold spread one cake with whipped cream and arrange strawberries cut into fan shapes over the cream, then place the other cake on top.

5 **To decorate:** Pipe rosettes of cream over the top of cake and decorate with fanned strawberries.

Right: Soaring over Victorian ranges. P.200-201: World famous Bondi Beach in Sydney. P.202-203: The Flinders Ranges, SA: P.204-205: Rottnest Island, Western Australia.

JUST DESSERTS

With tropical fruit from northern Queensland, Tasmania's King Island Cream, stone fruit of New South Wales, berries from Victoria and table grapes from South Australia, is it any wonder that we are a nation of sweet-tooths? Such is the range of our climate that this wonderful produce is available to us almost all year round.

Over the years, many of our tempting treats have become world famous. Take pavlova, for instance, or Peach Melba, both of which have become synonymous with this country. With such wonderful ingredients to work with our chefs can conjure up spectacular finales to any meal.

The home cook, too, can impress family and friends, with just a little imagination and this fine produce. Here we give you a selection of wonderful desserts for all seasons of the year. Some are ideal family fare, while others will make an impressive end to your next dinner party.

Left: The Grampian Mountains in Victoria.

Baked Strawberries and Almonds

2 tblspn slivered almonds

½ cup apricot jam

2 tblspn Grand Marnier

2 tspn sugar

2 punnets strawberries, hulled

1 Toast almonds on oven tray in moderate oven 5 minutes.

2 Warm jam, Grand Marnier and sugar in small saucepan.

3 Arrange strawberries in shallow ovenproof dish. Pour sieved jam mixture over strawberries.

4 Sprinkle almonds on top, bake in moderate oven 5 minutes or until heated through.

Serves 4

Passionfruit Souffle with Raspberry Yoghurt Sauce

½ cup passionfruit pulp

2 tblspn lemon juice

¾ cup icing sugar

6 eggwhites

RASPBERRY YOGHURT SAUCE

125g (4oz) frozen raspberries

200g (6½oz) carton low fat plain yoghurt

1 tblspn sugar

1 tblspn Grand Marnier

1 Place passionfruit pulp, lemon juice and half the icing sugar in a bowl, mix well. Beat eggwhites until soft peaks form, add remaining sifted sugar gradually and continue beating until firm peaks form.

Below: Baked Strawberries and Almonds

2 Gradually fold quarter of the eggwhites into passionfruit mixture, then fold in remaining eggwhites.

3 Lightly grease four individual souffle dishes (1 cup capacity). Sprinkle inside of each one with castor sugar, shake away excess. Spoon souffle mixture into dishes, bake in hot oven for 10 minutes or until risen and golden. Dust tops with sifted icing sugar immediately. Serve with Raspberry Yoghurt Sauce.

Raspberry Yoghurt Sauce:

4 To make Raspberry Yoghurt Sauce: Push raspberries through sieve to remove seeds. Combine raspberries with yoghurt, sugar and Grand Marnier.

Serves 4

Right: Inside the cellar at Seppelts winery in Victoria.

Chocolate Indulgence Cake

2 cups self-raising flour

1 cup plain flour

1 cup cocoa

3 cups castor sugar

250g (½lb) butter

1¾ cup milk

1 tblspn vanilla essence

½ cup cream

3 eggs

1 cup chopped pecan nuts

1 cup chocolate chips

1 cup halved raisins

1 Sift flours and cocoa into a large bowl, stir in sugar. Make a well in the centre, add butter, milk, vanilla and cream. Beat with an electric mixer for 7 minutes.

2 Add eggs one at a time, beat until dissolved between additions.

3 Stir in pecans, chocolate and raisins, mix well. Pour into a greased and base lined tube pan or angel food pan. Bake in moderately slow oven for 2 hours or until cooked through. Cool in pan for 15 minutes before turning onto wire rack.

4 Decorate as desired. We used strawberries, pecan nuts dusted with icing sugar and chocolate icing.

Serves 8

Raspberry, Kiwifruit and Banana Salad with Lime Dressing

1 cup raspberries

4 kiwifruit, peeled and sliced

2 bananas, peeled and sliced

1 tblspn fresh mint leaves

DRESSING

¼ cup fresh lime juice

1 tspn grated lime rind

2 tspn sugar

1 In a bowl combine the fruit and mint leaves.

2 In a small bowl combine lime juice, rind and sugar, stir until sugar has dissolved. Pour over fruit in bowl and gently toss.

Serves 4

Zabaglione

4 egg yolks

4 tblspn sugar

4 tblspn marsala

Savoiardi biscuits to serve

1 Place ovenproof bowl over saucepan with barely simmering water. With a hand-held electric mixer beat yolks, sugar and Marsala until thick and foamy, about 5 minutes. Do not overheat.

2 Take bowl off the heat and continue beating until the mixture has cooled a little. Serve in glasses with Savoiardi biscuits.

Serves 4

Below: Chocolate Indulgence Cake.

Hazelnut and Apple Dessert Cake

125g (4oz) butter

125g (4oz) castor sugar

2 eggs

45g (1½oz) ground hazelnuts

1 tspn instant coffee

1 tblspn milk

125g (4oz) self-raising flour

salt

500g (1lb) apples

2 tblspn apricot jam

½ lemon

icing sugar

1 Cream butter with sugar till light and fluffy. Separate eggs, combine yolks with butter and sugar.

2 Toast ground hazelnuts on baking tray in 190°C (375°F) oven till brown. Cool and add to butter mixture.

3 Warm milk, add coffee, dissolve. Sift flour, add pinch of salt. Whisk eggwhites till stiff. Fold flour into butter mixture with coffee, then fold in eggwhites lightly. Pour into greased cake pan, bake 30 minutes or till cake is firm. Turn out, cool.

4 Peel, core and slice apples. Combine with jam, grated rind of lemon and its juice, cook covered over low heat till apples are soft, but not mushy. Cool.

5 Split cake in half horizontally, place bottom on serving plate. Top with apple mixture, then cover with remaining cake. Dust with icing sugar.

Serves 6–8

Plum Mousse

825g (26½oz) can plums

3 tspn gelatine

⅛ tspn ground cinnamon

½ cup thickened cream

2 tblspn chopped walnuts (optional)

1 Drain plums, reserve ½ cup of juice. Sprinkle gelatine over juice, stir until combined, dissolve over saucepan of hot water.

2 Press plums through a sieve, stir in gelatine mixture, cinnamon and cream, mix well.

3 Spoon into serving dishes. Refrigerate until set. Sprinkle with chopped walnuts, if desired.

Serves 4

Kiwifruit Sorbet

6 kiwifruit

125g (4oz) raw sugar

1 cup water

juice of 2 large lemons

1 tspn lemon rind, grated

1 Peel kiwifruit, puree.

2 Combine sugar with water, boil 5 minutes, cool.

3 Combine kiwifruit puree with cooled syrup, lemon juice and rind. Freeze till mushy, remove and beat thoroughly. Freeze till set. Alternatively, sorbet can be made in an ice cream maker if available.

Serves 4

Left: Plum Mousse.

P.211: Panning for gold in New South Wales. P.212-213: Preparing the pasture in Murrurundi, NSW. Below: Fisherman's Wharf in Fremantle.

Tropical Fruit Flan

PIE CRUST

120g (4oz) plain flour

¼ tspn salt

3 tblspn margarine

¼ cup cold water

CUSTARD

1 cup liquid skim milk

1½ tblspn margarine

2 eggs

1 tblspn plain flour

3 tblspn sugar

1 tspn brandy essence

FRUIT TOPPING

¾ cup sliced fresh strawberries

½ cup fresh blueberries

2 medium peaches, peeled, pitted and sliced

1 kiwifruit, peeled and sliced

GLAZE

1 tspn arrowroot

⅓ cup apple juice (no added sugar)

1 tspn strawberry essence

2 tblspn sugar

1 To make the crust: In mixing bowl, combine flour and salt. Cut in margarine until mixture resembles coarse meal. Add water and mix thoroughly. Form dough into a ball.

2 Preheat oven to 200°C (400°F). Roll dough, forming a 23 cm (9 in) circle about 3 mm (⅛ in) thick. Fit dough into a 20 cm (8 in) pie plate and flute or crimp edges. Cover pastry with 23 cm (9 in) circle of foil. Using a fork, prick bottom and sides of pie shell through foil. Bake for 15 minutes. Remove foil and continue baking until lightly browned, about 10–15 minutes. Remove from oven. Cool.

Below: A natural bridge at Kalburri, Western Australia.

3 To make the custard: In a small saucepan, bring milk and margarine to the boil. Remove from heat. In a small bowl of an electric mixer, beat eggs and flour until thick and light-coloured. Add ¼ cup hot milk mixture to egg mixture. Stir to combine. Stir egg mixture into remaining hot milk in saucepan. Reduce heat to medium, cook, stirring constantly, until mixture thickens. Remove from heat, stir in remaining ingredients. Cool. Spoon cooled custard into cooled pie crust.

4 To make the fruit topping: Arrange fruit over custard.

5 To make the glaze: In a small saucepan, dissolve arrowroot in apple juice and cook, stirring constantly, until mixture is clear and thickened. Remove from heat and stir in remaining ingredients. Cool slightly. Using a pastry brush, spread glaze evenly over fruit. Cover and refrigerate until chilled, about 1 hour.

Serves 6

Lemon Mousse with Blueberry Sauce

BLUEBERRY SAUCE

2 cups blueberries

1/4 cup sugar

2 tblspn freshly squeezed lemon juice

4 large eggs at room temperature, separated

1/2 cup sugar

1/3 cup freshly squeezed lemon juice

1/3 cup freshly grated lemon rind

pinch of salt

2/3 cup thickened cream, chilled, whipped

1/2 cup blueberries, extra

1 To make blueberry sauce combine blueberries with sugar and lemon juice in processor or blender. Process until smooth. Sieve and place in serving bowl.

2 With an electric mixer beat egg yolks with 1/3 cup of sugar in a bowl until pale and thick, about 5 minutes. Add lemon juice and rind, beat another 2 minutes.

3 In another bowl beat eggwhites with a pinch of salt and remaining sugar until they hold soft peaks. Combine whites with yolks, fold in whipped cream carefully. Spoon into a crystal serving dish. Refrigerate 30 minutes, serve scattered with blueberries and Blueberry Sauce.

Serves 6

Chestnut Mousse

1 cup cream

2 cups milk

1 tblspn plain gelatine

1/4 cup warm water

4 egg yolks

1/4 cup sugar

485g (15½oz) can sweetened chestnut puree

1/2 cup sugar, extra

1 cup water, extra

3 eggwhites

pinch salt

1 Place cream in bowl, refrigerate 1 hour. Bring milk to boil, cool. Soften gelatine in water.

2 Beat egg yolks and sugar in top of double boiler till light. Set over hot, not boiling water. Stir in cooled milk. Cook till mixture coats back of a spoon, stirring constantly, about 15 minutes.

3 Stir in softened gelatine, remove from heat. Strain custard, stand at room temperature till mixture begins to set and is cool.

4 Mash chestnut puree till smooth, stir in cooled custard. Beat cream in chilled bowl till soft peaks form, fold gently into custard.

5 Combine sugar with water in small saucepan and cook over medium heat till sugar is dissolved. Continue cooking without stirring about 10 minutes.

6 Beat eggwhites with salt till stiff peaks form. Pour hot syrup into eggwhites in slow stream, combine gently. Fold eggwhite mixture into custard mixture. Spoon into serving bowl. Cover. Refrigerate till set, about 5 hours.

Serves 12

Above: Spectacular limestone formations. P.218-219: Eden, New South Wales.

White Chocolate Ice-Cream with Hazelnuts

SYRUP

1 cup water

¾ cup sugar

⅓ cup hazelnuts, peeled, finely chopped

6 egg yolks

2 tspn vanilla extract

315g (10oz) white chocolate, melted

2 cups cream

1 To make syrup combine water and sugar in a saucepan, bring to a boil, stirring constantly, boil 5 minutes. Cool slightly.

2 Place hazelnuts on oventray and roast in moderate oven about 10 minutes, until golden. Place on plate to cool.

3 In a food processor combine egg yolks and vanilla extract. Blend at high speed until light and fully. With machine running, pour in warm syrup, blend.

4 With machine running, add melted chocolate, blend well, then add cream. Pour into a bowl, cover and chill in refrigerator, 1 hour.

5 Pour chilled mixture in ice-cream maker and freeze according to manufacturer's instructions. When ice-cream has nearly frozen, add hazelnuts and continue freezing until desired consistency has been reached.

Makes about 4 cups

Coffee Praline Cheesecake

BASE

125g (4oz) plain sweet biscuits

¼ cup coconut

90g (3oz) butter, melted

FILLING

2 eggs, lightly beaten

300ml (½ pint) carton thickened cream

¼ cup sugar

1 tblspn gelatine

3 tblspn water

1 tblspn instant coffee powder

500 (1lb) cream cheese

½ cup thickened cream, extra, whipped

PRALINE

¾ cup sugar

¼ cup water

½ cup chopped pecan nuts

1 Combine biscuits, coconut and butter, press over base of a 23cm (9in) springform pan, refrigerate until set.

2 Combine eggs, cream and sugar in the top of a double saucepan, stir over simmering water until thickened slightly, remove from heat.

3 Sprinkle gelatine over water, stir well, add to hot egg mixture. Add coffee, stir well, cool.

4 Beat cream cheese in small bowl with electric mixer until smooth. Gradually add egg mixture, beat well between additions. Pour over biscuit base, refrigerate until set.

5 Combine sugar and water in a saucepan, stir constantly over heat until sugar dissolves. Bring to a boil without stirring, cook until syrup turns golden brown. Stir in pecans, pour over a lightly oiled baking tray, allow to set, chop finely.

6 Remove cheesecake from pan, spread with extra whipped cream, sprinkle with praline.

Serves 8

Left: A winemaker at work in Rutherglen, Victoria.

Above: Coffee Praline Cheesecake.

Iced Christmas Pudding

½ cup each sultanas, currants and chopped raisins

¼ cup each chopped glace cherries and mixed peel

¼ cup chopped glace pineapple

¼ cup brandy

1 litre (2 pints) vanilla ice-cream, softened

½ cup cream

½ cup toasted flaked almonds

¼ cup chocolate bits

strawberry sauce and strawberries to decorate (optional)

1 Mix fruits with brandy. Cover with plastic wrap and leave for several hours or overnight.

2 Place softened ice-cream and cream in a large bowl and stir in fruits, almonds and chocolate bits.

3 Spoon into a pudding basin (about 7-cup capacity) and cover with freezer wrap. Freeze until required.

4 Remove freezer wrap and immerse basin in hot – not boiling – water for 20 seconds. Unmould pudding onto a chilled serving plate and serve with custard or strawberry sauce, as pictured.

Serves 10–12

Apricot-Sherry Trifle

450 g (14 oz) pkt sponge rolls

½ cup sweet sherry, marsala or port wine

825 g (27 oz) can apricot halves, drained

2 cups prepared dairy custard

100 g (3 oz) pkt red jelly crystals, set in a shallow tin

300 ml (½ pint) carton cream

strawberries (or frozen berries) and chopped nuts to decorate

1 Cut sponge rolls into 1 cm (½ in) slices and use half the slices to line base and sides of a glass bowl. Sprinkle slices with half the sherry, marsala or port wine.

2 Arrange half the apricots on top of cake and cover with half the custard.

3 Chop jelly into cubes and sprinkle half over the custard. Place another layer of cake slices on top, moisten with remaining sherry, marsala or port wine. Add another layer of apricots, custard and jelly.

4 Beat cream until thick and fill a piping bag. Pipe cream in a lattice pattern over top of trifle and decorate with berries and chopped nuts. Chill until ready to serve.

Serves 6–8

Below: The dolphins of Monkey Mia in Western Australia. P.224-225: Autumn leaves in the central-west of New South Wales. P.226-227: The Sydney skyline at night. P.228-229: The sun sets on Poppet Head at Kalgoorlie in Western Australia.

Right: Iced Christmas Pudding.

AUSSIE ENTERTAINING

Australians love to entertain, whether it is at a barbecue, a beach picnic, a formal dinner party or simply with a few friends round for the evening.

We have such wonderful produce to choose from that creating an interesting menu is not difficult. Succulent seafood makes a perfect entree, lean beef, lamb or pork can form the basis of the main dish, accompanied by interesting vegetable dishes. And what better to finish the meal than fresh fruit and Australian cheeses?

Entertaining doesn't have to be a hassle if you prepare well in advance. Choose dishes that can be partially prepared the day before or at least in the morning of the party.

The recipes in this chapter are easy to cook and are sure to please your guests and make your evening's entertaining memorable.

Left: Rich farming country in the Narrabri district of New South Wales.

Chicken Stuffed with Pistachios and Green Peppercorns

1 x 1.5kg (3lb) chicken, boned

125g (4oz) pork and veal mince

125g (4oz) sausage mince

½ cup pistachio nuts

1 tblspn drained green peppercorns

1 onion, grated

1 cup fresh breadcrumbs

1 egg, lightly beaten

oil

CITRUS SAUCE

1 orange

1 cup orange juice

2 tblspn orange marmalade

1 tblspn redcurrant jelly

2 tspn French mustard

2 tblspn water

1 Lay chicken out, skin side down. Combine mince, nuts, peppercorns, onion, breadcrumbs and egg, place along one end of the chicken.

2 Roll chicken up, tucking in edges. Tie with string to hold chicken in shape, brush with oil. Wrap in foil.

3 Place chicken into a baking dish, bake in moderate oven for 45 minutes. Remove foil, brush chicken with oil. Bake further 30 minutes or until golden brown and cooked through. Serve sliced with hot Citrus Sauce.

4 To make Citrus Sauce: Peel orange with a vegetable peeler, shred peel finely, drop into a pan of boiling water, simmer 2 minutes, drain. Combine orange and lemon juice, marmalade, redcurrant jelly, mustard and water in a saucepan, bring to boil, reduce heat, simmer until sauce reduces by half, strain. Add shredded peel.

Serves 8

Potato and Avocado Bake

1kg (2lb) new potatoes

750g (1½lb) kumera (orange sweet potato)

¼ cup olive oil

2 tblspn fresh rosemary twigs

2 onions, thinly sliced

1 avocado, chopped

1 Cut potatoes and kumera into 3 cm (1¼in) chunks, toss in oil, rosemary and onion. Place into a baking dish, bake in moderately hot oven for 40 minutes or until tender and crisp, turning occasionally.

2 Place avocado over potatoes, bake further 10 minutes.

Serves 8

■ *Right: A potter at work.*

Below: Chicken Stuffed with Pistachios and Green Peppercorns with Potato and Avocado Bake, and Stir-fried Mushrooms and Capsicum (p.234).

Satay Prawns (Shrimp)

1½kg (3lb) uncooked king (large) prawns (shrimp)

½ cup crunchy peanut butter

1 cup water

2 tblspn sherry

1 tblspn light soy sauce

2 tblspn lemon juice

2 tspn grated fresh ginger

2 tblspn honey

1 clove garlic, crushed

2 tspn curry powder

1 tspn ground cumin

1 Peel prawns, leaving tail intact, remove back vein.

2 Combine remaining ingredients in a bowl, add prawns, stir well to coat, stand 1 to 4 hours in refrigerator.

3 Thread prawns onto skewers, grill for about 3 minutes on each side, brush occasionally with peanut marinade.

Serves 8

Right: Satay Prawns.
Below: Rainbow Ice-Cream Log.

Rainbow Ice-Cream log

2 litres (8 cups) rich vanilla ice-cream

90g (3oz) dark chocolate, melted

125g (4 oz) fresh or frozen raspberries, pureed

1 tblspn Grand Marnier

200g (6½oz) roll marzipan

⅓ cup caramel sauce

¾ cup thickened cream

1 scorched peanut bar, chopped

1 Line base and sides of a loaf pan with foil, bring foil 5 cm (2in) above rim.

2 Soften a little bit less than ⅓ of the ice-cream, beat in small bowl

3 Soften ⅓ of the ice-cream, beat in small bowl with electric mixer until smooth. Add combined pureed raspberries and Grand Marnier. Roll half the marzipan to cover chocolate chip ice-cream, pour over raspberry ice-cream, freeze until firm.

4 Soften remaining ⅓ ice-cream, beat in small bowl with electric mixer until smooth, add caramel sauce, beat until combined. Roll remaining marzipan to cover raspberry ice-cream, pour over caramel ice-cream, freeze until firm.

5 Turn out onto serving plate using the foil to help you. Decorate with whipped cream and chopped scorched peanut bar.

Serves 8

Stir-fried Mushrooms and Capsicum (Pepper)

60g (2oz) butter

1 onion, sliced

1 green capsicum (pepper), cut into strips

1 red capsicum (pepper), cut into strips

1kg (2lb) baby mushrooms

½ cup red wine

3 tspn Worcestershire sauce

¼ cup chopped chives

1 Melt butter in a frying pan, add onion and capsicum, stir-fry until tender.

2 Add mushrooms, wine and sauce, toss well, cover, simmer for 3 minutes or until mushrooms are tender. Spoon into serving bowl, sprinkle with chives.

Serves 8

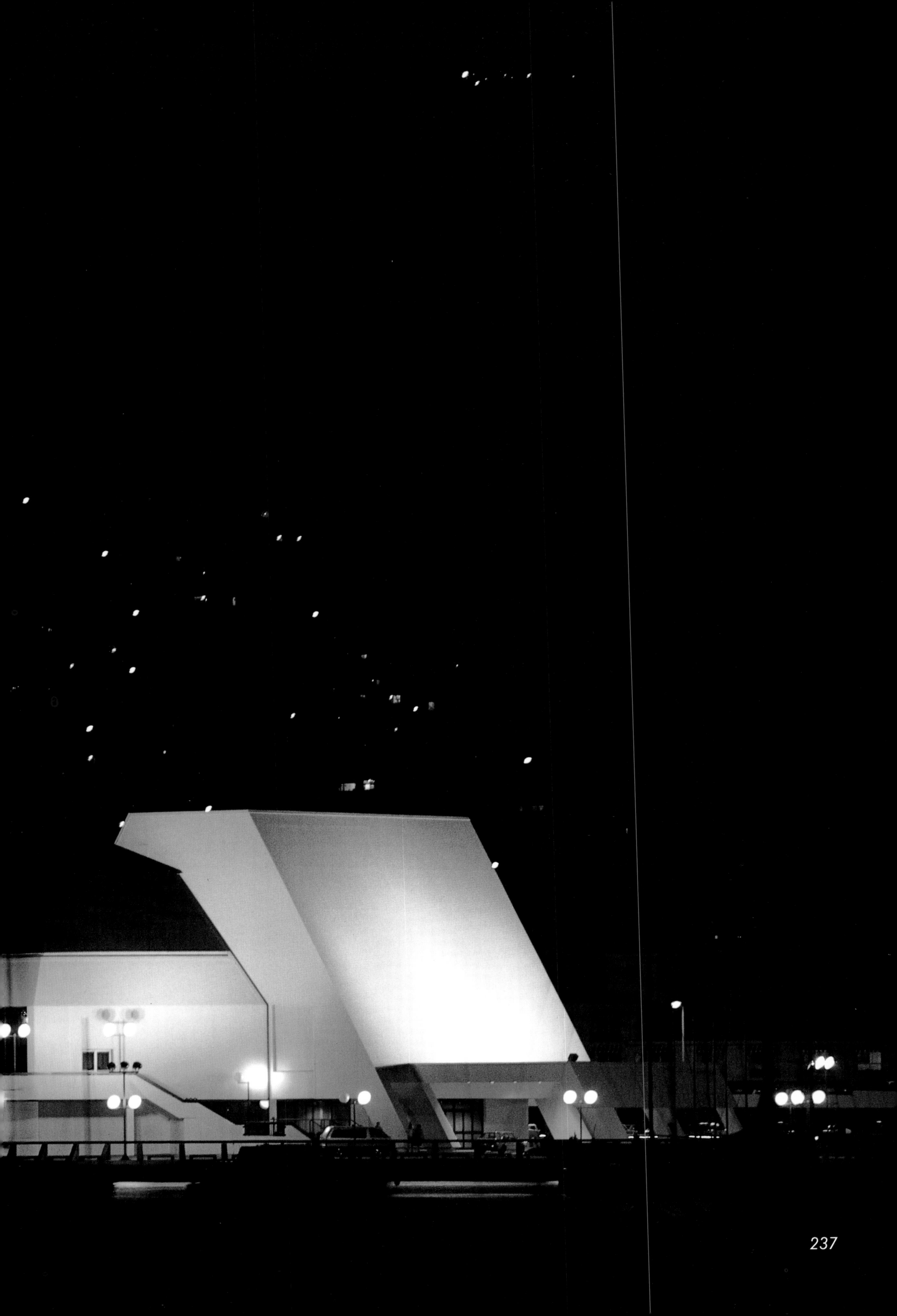

Curry and Cheese Stuffed Potatoes

8 potatoes

½ cup sour cream

4 spring onions (scallions), finely chopped

1½ tspn curry powder

1 tspn ground cumin

2 tspn lemon juice

¼ cup grated mature Cheddar cheese

1 Wash potatoes, cook in boiling water until tender, drain, cool.

2 Cut top from potatoes, reserve. Scoop potato from centre, mash well with a fork, stir in sour cream, spring onion, curry, cumin, lemon juice and cheese.

3 Spoon back into potatoes, replace lids. Bake in moderate oven 20 minutes or until heated through.

Serves 8

Artichoke and Tomato Salad

425g (13½oz) can artichoke hearts, drained

250g (½lb) punnet cherry tomatoes

3 oranges

4 Lebanese cucumbers

1 butter lettuce

2 tblspn chopped chives

DRESSING

½ cup olive oil

1 tblspn lemon juice

1 tblspn white vinegar

1 clove garlic, crushed

2 tspn chopped fresh oregano

1 tspn French mustard

1 Cut artichokes and tomatoes in half. Peel and segment oranges, slice cucumbers.

2 Line salad bowl with lettuce leaves. Combine prepared fruit and vegetables, spoon over lettuce.

Left: Chilled Roast Beef with Tarragon Bearnaise.

3 Combine all ingredients for dressing in a screwtop jar, shake well. Pour over salad, sprinkle with chives.

Serves 8

Chilled Roast Beef with Tarragon Bearnaise

1kg (2lb) eye fillet beef

1 tblspn cracked black pepper

2 tspn ground cardamom

2 cloves garlic, crushed

2 tblspn oil

TARRAGON BEARNAISE

1½ tblspn tarragon vinegar

1½ tblspn lemon juice

5 egg yolks

250g (½lb) butter

1 Remove fat and sinew from beef, tie with string to hold beef in shape during cooking. Roll beef in combine pepper, cardamom and garlic.

2 Heat oil in a baking dish, add beef, bake in hot oven for 20 minutes or until cooked as desired, turn beef occasionally. Allow to cool, serve sliced with Tarragon Bearnaise.

3 To make Tarragon Bearnaise: Simmer vinegar and lemon juice in a small saucepan until reduced to 2 tablespoons, cool. Blend or process egg yolks and vinegar mixture until frothy. With motor running gradually drizzle in hot, bubbly melted butter. Stand, covered at room temperature until required.

Serves 8

■ *P.236-237: The Hobart Casino.*

Port and Mushroom Liver Pate

500g (1lb) chicken livers

4 bacon rashers

125g (4oz) butter

1 onion, chopped

125g (4oz) mushrooms, chopped

2 cloves garlic, crushed

½ cup port

300ml (½ pint) carton thickened cream

Melba toast

1 Clean and trim chicken livers, chop roughly. Remove rind and fat from bacon, chop bacon roughly.

2 Melt butter in a frying pan, add onion, cook until tender. Add mushrooms, garlic, livers and bacon and port, cook for 10 minutes, stirring all the time.

3 Puree in a blender or processor with the cream until smooth. Pour into serving dish, refrigerate until firm. Serve with Melba toast.

Serves 8

Mango and Strawberry Pavlova

6 eggwhites

1¼ cup castor sugar

425g (13½oz) can mangoes, drained

1 tblspn Grand Marnier

½ cup thickened cream, whipped

½ cup cup sour cream

250g (½lb) punnet strawberries, halved

2 kiwifruit, sliced

1 passionfruit

1 small mango, sliced

1 Beat eggwhites in large bowl with electric mixer until soft peaks form. Gradually add sugar, beating until dissolved between additions. When all sugar is added, beat further 5 minutes.

2 Cut a 25cm (10in) circle of foil, place onto a greased baking tray. Grease and flour foil. Spread meringue evenly over foil, making the sides as straight as possible.

3 Bake in very slow oven 1½ hours or until firm to touch. Turn oven off, leave door closed, cool Pavlova in oven.

4 Carefully peel away foil, place Pavlova onto serving dish. Beat cream until soft peaks form. Puree canned mango until smooth, stir sour cream and Grand Marnier into mango, fold in cream.

5 Spread mango cream over Pavlova, decorate with strawberries, kiwifruit, passionfruit and mango slices.

Serves 8

P.242-243: *Bringing home the harvest.*

Left: Port and Mushroom Liver Pate. Below: Mango and Strawberry Pavlova.

Lamb Yoghurt Pilaf

750g (1½ lb) boneless lamb, cubed

juice of 2 lemons

¾ cup cream

½ cup natural yoghurt

1½ cups beef stock

4 whole cloves

1 tblspn butter, margarine or ghee

1 onion, finely chopped

1 tblspn poppy seeds

¼ tspn ground cardamom

½ cinnamon stick

2 bay leaves

4 spinach leaves, washed and shredded

1½ cups raw rice

extra ghee or butter

1 red capsicum (pepper), seeded and sliced

1 onion, sliced

1 Place lamb cubes in a large bowl. Add lemon juice, cream and yoghurt and stir until lamb is well coated with the cream mixture. Cover bowl with plastic wrap and refrigerate for at least 2 hours to allow the flavour to develop.

2 Place stock and cloves in a small saucepan and bring to the boil. Cover pan with a lid, lower heat and simmer for 5 minutes. Remove pan from heat and strain the liquid. Set liquid aside.

3 Melt butter, margarine or ghee in a deep, heavy-based saucepan. Add onion, poppy seeds and cardamom. Fry over moderate heat, stirring occasionally until onion has softened slightly, about 3 minutes.

4 Place cinnamon stick and bay leaves on a small square of muslin and tie up. Add to fried onion with meat, cream marinade, half a cup of the clove-flavoured stock and spinach. Mix well and bring to the boil. Cover pan with a lid, lower the heat and simmer gently for 1½ hours or until meat is tender.

5 Stir in the rice and remaining clove-flavoured stock and bring to the boil. Cover pan with a lid, lower the heat and simmer for 20 minutes or until rice is tender and most of the liquid has been absorbed. Remove muslin bag before serving. Garnish with pepper mixture.

6 Fifteen minutes before Pilaf is finished, melt ghee or butter in a heavy-based frying pan. Add onion and cook until golden, about 8-10 minutes.

Serves 6-8

Bamie Goreng

250g (½ lb) thin egg noodles

3 tblspn oil

1 clove garlic, crushed

1cm (½ in) piece fresh root ginger, finely chopped

2 chicken fillets, cut into strips

250g (½ lb) green prawns if available, or tinned shrimps, peeled and chopped

4 white cabbage leaves, shredded

1 stalk celery, sliced

3 carrots, peeled and sliced

salt and pepper

1 cup chicken stock

1 tblspn soy sauce

red chillies

1 Cook noodles in a saucepan of boiling salted water for 3 minutes. Drain, rinse under cold running water and drain again.

2 Heat oil in a large frying pan, add garlic and ginger and fry for 1 minute.

3 Add chicken and prawns and fry, stirring for 3 minutes or until chicken is white and prawns pink.

4 Add vegetables and cook, stirring constantly for a further 3 minutes.

5 Stir in noodles, salt and pepper to taste and stock and bring to the boil. Stir in soy sauce.

6 Pile onto a warm serving platter and garnish with chopped red chillies.

Serves 4

Right: A crisp morning on Mt. Baw Baw, Victoria. P.248-249: Lord Howe Island. P.250-251: Burning the canefields in Queensland. P.252-253: The Blue Mountains, New South Wales.

Left: Lamb Yoghurt Pilaf.

Spiced Pork Fillet

500g (1lb) pork fillet

1 tblspn tomato sauce

1 tblspn honey

1/8 tspn five spice powder

2 tspn soy sauce

1 tblspn honey, extra

SAUCE

1/2 cup chicken stock

1 tblspn dry sherry

1 tspn sugar

1/2 tspn oyster sauce

2 tspn cornflour

1 Marinate pork fillets in mixture of tomato sauce, honey, five spice powder and soy sauce for 30 minutes. Bake in moderate oven 20 minutes.

2 Brush fillets with extra honey on both sides, bake further 10 minutes.

3 Combine all ingredients for sauce in pan, cook until sauce boils and thickens. Cut pork into 1cm (1/2in) slices, serve with sauce.

Serves 4

Right: Spiced Pork Fillet.

Glazed Rack of Lamb

4 lean racks of lamb

1 tspn olive oil

1/3 cup lemon juice

1 tblspn soy sauce

1/3 cup honey

2 tspn rosemary

3/4 cup water

2 tblspn chopped mint

2 tblspn brown vinegar

1 tblspn sugar

2 tblspn water, extra

1 Combine oil, lemon juice, soy sauce and honey in large dish. Add racks lamb, turn to coat well with marinade, stand for 2 hours, turning occasionally.

2 Drain racks, reserve marinade for basting. Place rack in baking dish, brush with marinade. Sprinkle with rosemary. Bake in moderate oven for 45 minutes or until just cooked. Brush frequently with pan juices.

3 After 30 minutes, pour water in to prevent juices burning on bottom of pan. Remove racks when cooked, keep warm.

4 Place baking dish on top of stove, bring to boil, cook for 5 minutes. Add mint, vinegar, sugar and extra water, bring to boil, simmer for 2 minutes. Serve racks of lamb with sauce.

Serves 4

Pork Chops Dijon

4 lean pork loin medallions

1 tblspn olive oil

1 tblspn Dijon mustard

3 spring onions (scallions), chopped

2 tspn cornflour

1 cup beef stock

1 tblspn chopped parsley

1 Heat oil in pan, cook pork on both sides until golden brown. Add mustard and shallots. Stir well to mix with pan juices.

2 Add combined cornflour and stock. Bring to boil, stirring continually. Cook until mixture thickens. Reduce heat and simmer for 5 minutes or until pork is tender. Serve sprinkled with parsley.

Serves 4

Below: A pleasant lunch in the South Australian wine country.

INDEX

TEMPERATURE AND MEASUREMENT EQUIVALENTS

OVEN TEMPERATURES

	Fahrenheit	Celsius
Very slow	250°	120°
Slow	275–300°	140–150°
Moderately slow	325°	160°
Moderate	350°	180°
Moderately hot	375°	190°
Hot	400–450°	200–230°
Very hot	475–500°	250–260°

CUP AND SPOON MEASURES

Measures given in our recipes refer to the standard metric cup and spoon sets approved by the Standards Association of Australia.

A basic metric cup set consists of 1 cup, ½ cup, ⅓ cup and ¼ cup sizes.

The basic spoon set comprises 1 tablespoon, 1 teaspoon, ½ teaspoon and ¼ teaspoon. These sets are available at leading department, kitchen and hardware stores.

IMPERIAL/METRIC CONVERSION CHART

MASS (WEIGHT)
(Approximate conversions for cookery purposes.)

Imperial	Metric	Imperial	Metric
½ oz	15g	10oz	315g
1oz	30g	11oz	345g
2oz	60g	12oz (¾lb)	375g
3oz	90g	13oz	410g
4oz (¼lb)	125g	14oz	440g
5oz	155g	15oz	470g
6oz	185g	16oz (1lb)	500g (0.5kg)
7oz	220g	24oz (1½lb)	750g
8oz (½lb)	250g	32oz (2lb)	1000g (1kg)
9oz	280g	3lb	1500g (1.5kg)

METRIC CUP AND SPOON SIZES

Cup	Spoon
¼ cup = 60ml	¼ teaspoon = 1.25ml
⅓ cup = 80ml	½ teaspoon = 2.5ml
½ cup = 125ml	1 teaspoon = 5ml
1 cup = 250ml	1 tablespoon = 20ml

LIQUIDS

Imperial	Cup*	Metric
1floz		30ml
2floz	¼ cup	60ml
3floz		100ml
4floz	½ cup	125ml

LIQUIDS (cont'd)

Imperial	Cup*	Metric
5floz (¼ pint)		150ml
6floz	¾ cup	200ml
8floz	1 cup	250ml
10floz (½ pint)	1¼ cups	300ml
12floz	1½ cups	375ml
14floz	1¾ cups	425ml
15floz		475ml
16floz	2 cups	500ml
20floz (1 pint)	2½ cups	600ml

* Cup measures are the same in Imperial and Metric.

LENGTH

Inches	Centimetres	Inches	Centimetres
¼	0.5	7	18
½	1	8	20
¾	2	9	23
1	2.5	10	25
1½	4	12	30
2	5	14	35
2½	6	16	40
3	8	18	45
4	10	20	50
6	15		

NB: 1cm = 10mm.